FITNESS FOR SENIORS

50, 60 and Beyond

80 easy-to-follow illustrated home exercises to improve strength, balance, and energy

DAVID O'CONNOR

PREFACE

A fitness nut since my days at UCLA; cross-fit, trail running, and skiing are my passions. During the last twenty-five years as a Ski Instructor and PT, I've trained people of all ages to achieve their fitness goals.

A couple of years ago my father required assistance to improve his health, having become increasingly sedentary with each passing year. It took a sustained effort to get him to accept that it's never too late, and certainly not at only 65, to get fit. A simple but progressively challenging home exercise program was introduced and his eating habits modified.

Today, he lives a fulfilling active Californian lifestyle, regularly beating me on the golf course.

George Jedenoff is another source of inspiration; still skiing Snowbird at the age of 102. George attributes a daily exercise program plus a positive mindset for this vitality.

In this book, I share my knowledge to help seniors seeking to regain fitness, strength, and live a healthy active life but are unsure how to start. Follow the suggestions and exercises in this book and you will enjoy a higher quality of life.

David O'Connor

CONTENTS

FREE BONUS FITNESS MATERIAL TO HELP YOU

To ensure you get as much value as possible from Fitness For Seniors, I've put together some additional free bonus materials to help you achieve your goals, including:

- Weekly Workout Plans provided as printable PDF documents.
- As a bit of fun to help maintain brain fitness too, 4 fitness Word Puzzles.
- Monthly email Newsletter on topics to help you succeed on your fitness journey.
- An exciting surprise bonus currently being prepared, I'll email you when it's ready

To get instant access to your free bonus material, go here now: www.iaa.pub/bonus

INTRODUCTION

Getting older is a part of life, and as we age our bodies start to change. Often, these changes begin much earlier than we realize. We develop different dietary needs, and experience changes to our muscular and skeletal systems. Activities that were once easy, like climbing stairs or gardening, may become painful and difficult.

While genetics plays an important role in our health as we age, a lot of how our bodies handle the aging process has to do with lifestyle choices we can control. For example, as the years pass, we may gradually reduce our level of physical activity to the point where we become comfortable living a sedentary lifestyle, which carries considerable risk because of the well-documented health issues associated with such a lifestyle. The sooner we start making key changes to habits such as nutrition and exercise, the better the chances we have of enjoying active, healthy lives in our golden years.

The best news about getting older is how much control you have over your experience. *Fitness for Seniors* is a kind of travel guide for the aging process. Here, you will learn what changes are happening in your body and how to adapt to these changes to live your best life as you get older.

You will also find easy-to-follow explanations of the suggested specific lifestyle changes. The two biggest areas you will need to focus on are nutrition and exercise if you want to enjoy a high quality of life no matter how old you live to be. Studies show that even a moderate level of physical activity can have a huge impact on your quality of life as you age. Similarly, your body needs different nutrients than it did when you were younger. You cannot continue to eat and exercise the same way you did before if you want to be fit, active and healthy in your golden years.

It is important that you have the right information within your reach, with easy ways to keep your body active, to keep you feeling strong and confident. *Fitness For Seniors* provides exactly that, encouraging you to commit to small changes today that will positively impact all of your tomorrows.

If you can spare a minute please be sure to leave a short Amazon review. I'll be checking the reviews personally and your feedback will help others on their fitness journey.

To Leave A Review:

You can visit **www.iaa.pub/review** and you'll be automatically taken to Amazon to leave a review.

or

use Amazon's link to Fitness For Seniors Page: **https://www.amazon.com/Fitness-Seniors-Beyond-easy-follow-ebook/dp/B0B9CKQ275#customerReviews** and then click on the "**Write a customer review**." button

or

scan the QR code:

HOW TO USE THIS BOOK

Because this book is a guide, you may want to skip around to different parts that are most applicable to your needs. Below is a summary of the various elements of the book.

The first chapter focuses on diet and nutrition. In the second chapter, you will learn the basics of developing a healthy exercise routine. This portion of the book is designed for beginners who are not currently exercising or are exercising very little, and for those that wish to refresh their knowledge.

In chapter six, you will find several workout routines that focus on different areas such as stretching, cardio, upper body, lower body, and core strength, to make exercising easy while helping push you closer to achieving your fitness goals. These exercises require little to no equipment and come with colorful illustrations to guide you through the process.

If you already enjoy an active life, you may want to skip ahead to chapter six and the chapters that follow.

Getting older can be the most incredible adventure of your life. You have the opportunity to explore new places, ideas, things, and people. *Fitness For Seniors* is here to give you the knowledge to maintain strength, mobility, and vitality in order to live life on your own terms.

Let's get started!

WHAT YOU WILL LEARN

- The relationship between nutrition and exercise.
- The part exercise plays in the prevention and management of some age-related health conditions.
- How to keep yourself motivated and on track even on days when you don't feel like it.
- The various types of equipment you can use as you start your fitness journey.
- Alternatives around the home you can use for exercising.
- Various exercises you can do to target specific parts of your body.
- Safety protocols every senior should follow.
- How to manage the intensity of the exercises depending on your fitness level.
- What it takes to create an exercise routine for yourself.
- How you can keep the momentum going long after the eight-week program.

Having a life where you can trust your body to do what you need it to and go about your day in high spirits with positive energy is within your grasp. All it takes is to be willing to do what is necessary to get there.

CHAPTER 1:

THE PART NUTRITION PLAYS

As you age, your body undergoes some changes. You will experience muscle loss, reduced ability to sense when you are hungry or thirsty, less stomach acid to digest food and absorb nutrients, eating fewer calories, and more. The issue with some of these changes is that they create nutritional problems for the body.

Good nutrition is important for the body's well-being at any age, but as an older adult, the need for proper nutrition becomes more important. It serves as a way to prevent deficiency related diseases and control the risk of non-communicable health conditions like high blood pressure, type 2 diabetes, and heart disease. When combined with exercise, nutrition can help the body repair macromolecular damage, prevent obesity, and reduce the risk of age-related diseases.

On the other hand, eating foods that don't contain the nutrients your body needs can increase the aging process due to uncontrolled oxidative stress. For instance, if you do not get enough vitamin C and E in your meals, your body may experience an increase in free radicals because these vitamins are important in creating antioxidants, which prevent free radicals from developing. To confirm this, the

Academy of Nutrition and Dietetics noted that up to 70% of health decline in older adults with chronic diseases is caused by risk factors such as poor nutrition (Bernstein & Munoz, 2012).

As a result, older adults who eat fewer calories and nutrients can experience unexpected weight loss and dehydration, which can have severe consequences on their well-being.

Therefore, before you begin any of the exercises in this book, it is important that you remember the place of nutrition and that having a healthy balanced diet is what you need to take your health to the next level. If you already have a healthy diet, you can maintain it, or modify it due to changing nutritional needs depending on recommendations given by your doctor. If you don't have a healthy diet or meal plan, make sure to talk to your doctor about your desire to increase your physical activity, and which nutrients you should consume more of. Since we are on the topic of nutrients, let's take a look at some nutrient-rich foods that will help you look and feel your best in the years ahead.

16 Nutrients & Foods That Help with Healthy Aging

Nutrients

Since your body needs fewer calories, the goal is to eat nutrient dense foods and cut out as many empty calories as possible. Before we get into food, here are some vitamins and minerals that you should focus on including in your diet:

Iron

Older adults have higher risks of anemia caused by iron deficiency; eating foods that are rich in iron preserves energy levels, regulates body temperature, helps increase the immune system, and aids with gastrointestinal activity.

Protein

Seniors are encouraged to eat more protein to reduce the loss of muscle mass and strength. This loss of muscle mass and strength is called sarcopenia, and when it is not managed, it can lead to poor quality of life or physical disabilities.

Taking an increased amount of protein via diet or protein supplements helps to reduce loss of muscle mass, and when combined with exercise, it can help the body in building more muscle. Studies from the National Institute of Health found that adults who ate more protein lost less muscle mass than those who ate smaller amounts.

Magnesium

This supports the immune system, assists with muscle function, helps balance blood glucose levels, and aids in protein synthesis. Unfortunately, many older adults are deficient in this mineral because of their medications or changes in gut function.

If you have low levels of magnesium, you should consider including some magnesium rich foods in your diet. To find out if you have magnesium deficiency, watch for symptoms such as shaking, muscle spasms, loss of appetite, nausea or vomiting, fatigue, and hyper-excitability.

Vitamin B12

This vitamin is needed for the production of red blood cells and healthy brain function. Vitamin B12 can be found in some of the proteins you eat, but older people with a reduction in the production of stomach acid may not have sufficient amounts of B12 in their system because their bodies cannot separate it from the proteins in their diet.

A study published in 2013 noted this, as it estimates that about 10-30% of adults over the age of 50 cannot properly absorb vitamin B12 from their meals (Allen, 2012).

Also, vegetarians who do not consume animal proteins—which are rich sources of this vitamin–can turn to B12 supplements, or foods fortified with B12, to increase its amount in their bodies.

Calcium and Vitamin D

Calcium and vitamin D are two important nutrients needed to make bones strong and healthy. However, as you grow older your body may find it difficult to absorb calcium from foods, and experience a decrease in the ability to manufacture its own vitamin D. If you are deficient in either of these nutrients, you are more susceptible to loss of bone density, which can result in fractures.

So, what can you do about this? The best thing to do is to get more of these nutrients from supplements like cod liver oil, and from foods that are rich in calcium and vitamin D like spinach, kale, okra, soybeans, and foods fortified with them, such as oatmeal or orange juice.

Fiber

Due to some medications or reduced physical activity, you may experience constipation more frequently than you would like. Eating foods rich in fiber is one way to relieve constipation because they promote regular bowel movements and allow waste products to pass more easily through the body.

In addition, a high fiber diet can help to prevent diverticular disease, which is caused by a low fiber, high fat diet.

Foods

Following are some of the nutrients you should consider when planning your meals, and you can find them in these foods which promote good health.

Green Tea

Free radicals are a product of cell functioning and can also form due to some aspects of our environment, like UV light. They are unstable and can harm your cells if nothing is done to control them.

Green tea contains antioxidants that can stabilize free radicals and reduce their ability to cause cell damage. In addition, stabilizing these molecules minimizes the risk of cancer, heart disease, premature aging, and other chronic diseases linked to free radicals.

Fish

Most fish, especially fatty fish, can help with healthy skin. They are rich in collagen and elastin, two proteins responsible for making your skin plump, firm, and elastic.

Omega-3 fat is another nutrient present in fish that is immensely beneficial to older adults because they fight against heart disease and can stand in the way of inflammation that damages the skin. In addition, the presence of selenium in fish plays a part in DNA synthesis, reducing the effects of UV light on the skin, and the severity of some skin diseases such as psoriasis.

Extra Virgin Olive Oil

Filled with antioxidants like beta carotene, tocopherols, phenolic compounds, and healthy fats, extra virgin olive oil is a healthy addition to any diet. Its antioxidants and nutrients place it in a unique position to help with oxidative damage, inflammation, and skin aging. In addition, the risk of chronic diseases like heart disease, some types of cancer, and type 2 diabetes are reduced by olive oil.

Vegetables

It's already common knowledge that vegetables are a great addition to any diet for several reasons. They contain antioxidants that protect the body against cataracts, heart disease, and some types of cancer. Most vegetables contain reasonable amounts of beta-carotene and lycopene that help with premature aging by minimizing the effects of UV rays on the body.

Since they contain high amounts of vitamin C, making vegetables a part of your meals increases collagen production in the body and gives your skin a healthy look.

Dark Chocolate

It contains flavanols, polyphenols, and other antioxidants that lower the risk of cognitive decline and heart disease. The nutrients present in dark chocolate can slow down skin aging and protect from sun damage.

There are different varieties of dark chocolate, and you can find options that contain little to no added sugar to add to your diet.

Milk and Yogurt

The World Health Organization encourages adults above the age of 50 to take about 1200mg of calcium daily to strengthen their bones and prevent osteoporosis (Aging.

com, 2017). You can easily get your daily dose of calcium from milk and yogurt that are rich in calcium.

Plus, foods fortified with calcium like almond and soy milk are excellent additions to your diet, and you can combine them with supplements recommended by your doctor.

Nuts, Wholegrain Bread, and Fruits

These are excellent sources of fiber that help with regular bowel movement and prevent heart disease. If nuts and some fruits are too difficult to chew, you can go for nut pastes, vegetables, and softer fruits like oranges, bananas, berries, passion fruit, and grapefruits that are high in fiber.

Plus, these fruits are good sources of magnesium and potassium, both of which are important for physiological functions in the body.

Avocados

Avocados are an excellent source of healthy fats—they contain vitamins, minerals, and antioxidants. The nutrients present in avocados promote skin health, and fight against free radicals that can increase skin aging and cell damage.

Tomatoes

With their high levels of antioxidants such as lycopene, especially when paired with healthy fats like avocados, tomatoes have several health benefits.

They reduce the risk of chronic diseases like diabetes mellitus, heart complications, and health conditions caused by oxidative stress. The presence of lycopene provides a layer of protection against skin damage by sunlight.

Water

As you get older, you may not feel as thirsty as you used to, but your body still needs plenty of water to function properly. A study conducted by researchers from Tufts University notes that drinking up to 8 glasses of water is just as important as physical activity for older adults (Lichtenstein et al., 2008).

To increase your water intake, take some of it along with you in a small container so that you can always have some water close to you. However, for seniors with liver or kidney disease, it is advisable to consult your doctor first about the amount of water appropriate for you.

Foods That You Should Avoid Eating

It would help if you were cautious of some food choices because of how they can interact with certain medications, and the possibility of developing some food-related diseases from them. The foods that you should be cautious of, or avoid eating entirely if possible are:

Raw or Undercooked Foods

Raw or undercooked eggs, meat, fish, and raw seafood in general should be avoided by seniors. They carry with them an increased risk of Salmonella food poisoning and other harmful bacteria like Listeria, E.coli, and Campylobacter.

Eating raw seafood like mussels and oysters can be a bit risky for older adults as they can lead to dehydration, vomiting, and diarrhea. So, foods like sushi that use mostly raw food items should be avoided. But you can eat the cooked varieties of sushi if they are accessible to you.

All foods you eat should be properly cooked to ensure that any bacteria that can cause food poisoning or other illnesses are removed from them.

Unpasteurized Milk and Juice

Unpasteurized milk and fruit juice are typically considered healthy because all their nutrients are left intact, but they may not be such a healthy option for older adults. Unpasteurized milk and juice contain bacteria that would have been killed during pasteurization and thus increase the risk of disease.

This doesn't mean that you should stay away from milk and juice altogether, as these beverages still contain some incredible nutrients.

Multigrain Bread

Multigrain bread is not entirely bad for seniors, but it's important to look at the ingredients list before purchasing. If it is made with high fructose corn syrup, then it's best to avoid it.

Sprouts

Sprouts are generally regarded as a superfood because of their many vitamins and minerals, but they can be a breeding ground for harmful bacteria. E.coli and salmonella can get trapped in the seeds as they sprout, and when consumed, can result in pneumonia and weight loss that can be dangerous to your health.

You can still get just as many vitamins and minerals from other leafy greens.

Sugary Drinks

Drinks like soda might seem like a great option to satisfy your sweet tooth, but regular consumption of sugary drinks can lead to obesity, diabetes, tooth decay and other health issues.

Alcoholic Drinks

Drinking the occasional glass of wine or other alcoholic beverage is usually harmless, but you should avoid alcohol if you have diabetes, take painkillers, antihistamines, or any high blood pressure medication.

Verdict

Maintaining proper nutrition as a senior can be a bit challenging for several reasons. You may start to experience difficulty eating or begin to have issues getting around because you live alone. Financial constraints can also make it tough to talk to a nutritionist or doctor, and you may not be able to spend as much on food. When faced with these challenges, it is important to remember that it's the *quality* of the food—not the quantity—that counts.

Avoid over processed foods with empty calories like chips and candy and focus on foods that are packed with the nutrients that your body needs. If you live alone and find it difficult to eat healthy, you could try enjoying some meals at a senior center close to you and enjoy the feeling of having company.

For seniors who find it difficult to chew, have a dentist check for problems, and discuss recommendations that will make eating easier. If this isn't an option, try drinking more liquids such as fortified juices, or grazing on smaller meals or snacks throughout the day instead of sitting for one main meal.

Above all, don't forget to combine your new healthy eating plan with physical activity to optimally improve your health.

Key Points

- Increasing your physical activity is good, but combining it with quality nutrition makes it even better.
- Since seniors require fewer calories, more emphasis should be placed on eating quality, nutrient-dense foods that improve quality of life.
- If you can, it's important that you seek the advice of your doctor or nutritionist before starting or changing your meal plan. Depending on the health issues you're facing, you may get some useful food and supplement recommendations specific to your evolving individual needs.

Starting Strong

- Check out the Dietary Guidelines for Americans and note the recommended daily nutrition for seniors (USDA, 2020a).
- See how you can incorporate their recommendations into your diet, and make sure to share that information with close family members, and your caregiver (if applicable). Ensuring everyone is on the same page will greatly help to ensure any changes needed to your lifestyle will happen, and stick in the long run.

CHAPTER 2:

EXERCISING AND HEALTH

The aging process is a complex one, and for a long time, there has been a lot of interest in understanding how it works. Aging is typically associated with characteristics such as increased frailty, risk of communicable disease, reduced sensitivity to nutritional needs, cell deterioration, and a general decline in the body's physiological functions.

While medications, treatments, and special diets are available to keep older adults in prime shape as they age, studies show that exercise is an exceptional natural remedy for reversing the cellular damage accumulated during a person's lifespan, slowing down the aging process. How does this work? Let's see what science has found before going into the benefits of exercise.

In 1966, researchers at the University of Texas Southwestern Medical School conducted a study with five 20-year-old men. These men were asked to stay in bed for three weeks with no physical activity—when they were tested three weeks later, the results were shocking. These healthy men developed characteristics common in 50-year-old men like high blood pressure, increased resting heart rate, decreased muscle strength and mass, and a slight decrease in the heart's pumping capacity. Luckily, these changes were reversed after eight weeks of exercising (McGavock et al., 2009).

Fast forward 30 years; these same men, now 50 years old, underwent the same study again. They were experiencing some decline in their physiological functions at that age such as high blood pressure, so asking them to go on bed rest for three weeks was risky. Instead, the University of Texas researchers asked them to start exercising, and created a six-month plan for them that included various forms of exercise. After the program, the men lost some of their excess body weight, but their heart rates, blood pressures, and heart maximum pumping capacity returned to the way they were at 20 years of age. This research is one of the major studies that help us understand the effects of exercising on aging (McGavock et al., 2009).

With technological advancements, our society is becoming more sedentary than it used to. There is practically no need to move around when you have a car to take you anywhere you need to go, a caretaker attending to your pressing needs, and food delivered to you if you need it, but no one feels the effects of having a sedentary lifestyle more than older adults, as it makes you sensitive to health risks even with the presence of medications and treatments.

Exercise can affect your body by:

- **Improving bone density:** The body replaces old bone tissue with new ones to keep your bones strong, but as you approach your 40s and 50s, your body's ability to do this starts to decline, which is why seniors tend to lose more bone mass as they age.

  The more bone mass the body loses, the greater the risk of osteoporosis, a disease that causes bones to break easily. While you cannot gain more bone mass as an older adult, regular exercise like aerobics and walking can maintain existing bone mass and, by extension, prevent bone loss.

- **Preventing Disease:** Exercise strengthens the immune system and helps to prevent diseases like diabetes and heart disease. As a senior your immune system can easily be compromised, so to provide support to your body, regular exercise is imperative.
- **Increasing Energy Levels:** Exercise puts you in a good mood by increasing energy levels, allowing you to be more involved in social activities. It will give you the strength to do what you love without feeling tired easily, giving you a sense of purpose, happiness, and satisfaction.
- **Lengthens Telomeres:** Telomeres are the end of each chromosome. They shorten as a person grows older; inadequate exercise, obesity, and stress can contribute to this. Cells with shorter telomeres cannot replicate, which increases the risk of chronic and infectious diseases like stroke, heart disease, high blood pressure, tissue damage, and increased signs of aging. Increasing your level of physical activity combined with other factors like stress management, diet, and social support, is a good way to lengthen your telomeres and protect your health.
- **Improving Cognitive Function:** Mental abilities like learning, thinking, problem-solving, decision making, memory, and attention are all aspects of cognitive function. As you grow older, the ability to perform one cognitive task to the other and process information quickly declines. When your cognitive function is impaired, you may experience memory loss, poor reasoning and judgment, language and attention problems, and a general decline in your mental abilities. Unfortunately, mild cognitive impairment is more com-

mon in older adults. The American Academy of Neurology estimates that approximately 8% of seniors between the ages of 65-69 suffer mild cognitive impairment. This percentage increases to 37% in seniors 85 years of age and older (Peterson et al., 2017).

What can be done to help? While there are exercises that can help improve a person's cognitive function, moderate physical activity can reduce mild cognitive impairment as it improves balance, mobility, and daily functions in older adults.

Exercise and Sarcopenia

We have over 600 muscles present in every part of our body. The muscular system is a complex and important one because it plays a crucial role in how our body functions. What functions do our muscles perform?

Muscles help with mobility and stability: The muscles in your body help with coordinated movements like walking and running, as well as simple motions like writing and facial movements. In addition, our strong skeletal muscles are responsible for keeping us stable and standing tall.

Muscles aid blood circulation: The cardiac muscles in the heart are responsible for pumping blood throughout the body by receiving electrical signals. The muscles in the veins and arteries also have a part to play, as they maintain blood pressure and circulation even when there is blood loss or an increased need for oxygen. For instance, when exercising, the veins and arteries will expand to increase blood circulation and give the body the oxygen it needs.

Muscles help with digestion: There is a class of muscle called smooth muscles located in the gastrointestinal tract, and these help to push food from the esophagus to the stomach.

The muscles in the stomach allow it to process food properly, and when it moves to the intestine, the muscles present there help the food to pass out of the body as a waste product.

Muscles protect the body from fatal injuries: Muscles provide a form of cushioning to your internal organs, bones, and joints, reducing the possibility of internal injuries and fatal conditions.

As you grow, your muscles are designed to grow with you, so you feel completely fine in your teenage years and 20s, even with minimal physical activity. But this changes when you approach the 3rd decade of your life. In your 30s, your body starts to lose some muscle strength and mass, but these effects may not be felt right away. Instead, this loss in muscle mass and strength continues to build until it results in sarcopenia.

Sarcopenia is a common condition affecting older adults, and it happens due to muscle degeneration. It is more visible in adults above the age of 50, and it reduces a person's ability to go about their daily activities. Plus, it is believed that it affects 30% of adults over the age of 60, and 50% of adults over the age of 80. This condition can happen for several reasons.

First on the list is inadequate physical activity or having a sedentary lifestyle. When you don't use your muscles enough or do anything to make them stronger, it can increase the rate of muscle loss, and make it difficult to maintain existing muscle mass.

Having a poor diet is another factor that can contribute to sarcopenia. When your body doesn't have the required calories or nutrients, it can reduce muscle mass and promote unexpected weight loss. Also, when a person experiences chronic illness, it can affect the body's ability to properly tear down and heal damaged cells and, by extension, retain muscle mass.

There is no specific test for percentage of muscle mass to determine if a person has sarcopenia, but doctors can diagnose it based on the symptoms an individual has. The patient usually has to undergo a dual-energy X-ray absorptiometry (DXA) test to determine the lean muscle mass of the affected individual. If it is lower than what is expected for an average person of the same age, it can be taken as a sign of sarcopenia.

To get further information, the patient may be asked to do a walking test to determine their average gait speed, and a handgrip strength test to measure their muscle strength. The reports from these tests help diagnose sarcopenia in older adults.

When you have sarcopenia, it can be a bit difficult to do the things you want. You gradually become weaker and can't move as much as you did. The smallest tasks make you feel tired or worn out, and you develop an increasing disinterest in social activities. You'll experience decreased muscle balance, become prone to fractures and aches, and become less resistant to insulin, increasing the risk of hospitalization or disability.

Sarcopenia gradually reduces quality of life, but the good news is you don't have to wait to feel its full effects before finding ways to slow it down, and the best way to do that is through exercise.

In 2012, the University of Sydney conducted a study using seniors 70 years or older to determine the impact of exercise on muscle mass and strength. These seniors were made to do high-intensity resistance training exercises, and at the end of the program, they all saw an increase in muscle mass which positively impacted their overall health (Clemson et al., 2012).

Since there are no pharmaceutical drugs or medical treatments available for sarcopenia, the best way to slow it down is to improve the quality of your muscles through physical activity, but not all exercises are equal when it comes to managing sarcopenia.

The best exercises are strength and resistance training because they increase the strength of your muscles as well as the activity of growth-promoting hormones, which helps muscle cells to grow and heal when damaged. Other forms of exercise like aerobic activity such as cardio workouts can be included to improve overall health.

The Connection Between Exercise and Nutrition

There is an undeniable, unshakeable connection between exercise and nutrition; regardless of your health and fitness goals, one cannot be done without the other.

Nutrition fills your body with the nutrients it needs to function. Without a healthy diet, you may face health issues like obesity and dementia. A poor diet can also affect your mental health and ability to engage in physical activities.

Exercise helps burn the calories you consume and allows the body to effectively use the available nutrients. For instance, the body will be unable to make use of proteins or other muscle-growing nutrients when you are not putting your muscles to work, because there is nothing to grow or heal.

Exercise is also a good way to manage stress and improve your mood, reducing the risk of heart disease and other chronic diseases like some types of cancer. Furthermore, it helps to improve blood circulation and stabilizes sugar and insulin levels. In addition, exercising regularly is important for better sleep, improved cognitive performance, and higher quality of life.

Why are we discussing this relationship between food and exercise? The problem is that some people still see the connection between the two as transactional. They workout so that they won't feel guilty about eating junk food or their general eating habits. Some also believe that doing one without the other is enough for them to stay healthy or maintain an average level of fitness, but the two intertwined together are the key to living a healthy life.

The individual benefits of both good nutrition and exercise are enhanced when you make both a part of your lifestyle. For instance, your body needs good sources of calcium like milk, cheese, and green leafy vegetables for healthy bones, but that cannot fully be achieved without exercises like strength training. Its impact may not be felt right away, but your body will thank you in the long run.

Also, it is important to remember that increasing your level of physical activity doesn't stop after a 10-20 minute workout. It includes all the daily activities that help your body lose calories and stay fit, whether small or big. These types of activities are called Non-Exercise Activity Thermogenesis (NEAT).

To make the most out of NEAT, it is important to increase your daily movement. For example, take a casual walk in the evening or morning when you can, go to the grocery store instead of ordering takeout, and do some random movements when you notice that you've been sitting for a while. These small movements, combined with regular exercise and a good diet make the difference.

Myths and Misconceptions about Exercising for Seniors

Were you already giving up on the thought of exercising because you believe that there is nothing it can do for you as an older person? Or do you, like many others, believe that you are just too old or out-of-shape to exercise? In this section, we will be discussing some of the misconceptions older adults have about exercising, and why they hold no water. However, the main point is 'You are never too old or unfit to start.'

Myth 1: Exercising or staying healthy at my age is pointless

This is probably one of the strongest misconceptions older adults have about exercise. Since aging is typically associated with physiological decline, they believe that nothing can be done to improve their health, and can only maintain it with medications, but that is far from the truth.

Regular exercise can improve your muscle and bone strength, protect your mental health, and reduce the risk of Alzheimer's disease, which enables you to maintain your independence. When you exercise with other people, it helps you to socialize and increase your confidence. When you can keep doing the things you love as you grow older, it helps you live a happy and fulfilled life.

Myth 2: Exercising is not safe for me

Like many other myths we'll be shattering, there is no element of truth in this one. Older adults have a higher chance of falling due to accidents, imbalance, and poor movement patterns, but studies have shown that the risk of falling and sustaining injuries is greatly reduced when you exercise.

Strength training and stability exercises are a great way to improve your balance, and stave off the risk of weak bones and osteoporosis.

Myth 3: I cannot exercise without the supervision of a physician

According to the guidelines released by the American College of Sports Medicine in 2009, an adult does not need a doctor's approval before exercising as long as they are healthy and reasonably capable of doing it.

But where you have an underlying disease or health condition, it is advisable to check with your physician before starting any form of exercise. If you are recovering from an illness or a risky event like falling and a fracture, you may need some form of supervision for your safety and guidance.

When doing it alone, it is best to start slowly and focus more on your posture and form. As you get comfortable with it, you can gradually increase your speed while remaining safe.

Myth 4: Water-based exercises are the only type I should focus on

Older adults favor water-aerobics for several reasons. The water provides enough support to reduce injuries, especially when you have underlying health conditions like high blood pressure. Water-based exercises are considered safe, and they yield almost the same health benefits as other types of exercises.

There is no problem if you enjoy this type of exercise above others, but you can always combine land-based exercises for better results. You can use the modified alternatives for these exercises or decrease their intensity to suit your goals. Plus, having a wide variety of exercises to choose from makes it fun.

Myth 5: I cannot afford to exercise

You don't need to go to a gym or buy expensive home equipment like treadmills before you can exercise—sometimes, it doesn't have to cost anything.

Walking is a form of exercise, and you don't need to pay anyone or buy any special equipment before you do it. For more complex exercises, all you may need is a comfortable surface for you to lie on, or a chair to support your movements.

For weight training, you can substitute water bottles instead if you do not have the funds to get hand-weights. Exercising doesn't have to cost much, and you can always modify it based on your needs. What's important is that you never give yourself a reason to stop moving.

Myth 6: There is no time to exercise

This is a common misconception among all age groups. The World Health Organization recommends that older adults should do at least 150 minutes of moderate aerobic physical activity or 75 minutes of vigorous physical activity in a week, and this can seem like a lot. But if you divide the time for six days, assuming that you want to take one day off to rest, it comes down to 25 minutes of exercise per day, which isn't much. If you don't have time to exercise for 20-25 minutes at once, you can always split the time. For instance, you can do moderate or high-intensity exercises for 10-15 minutes in the morning, and round it up with an evening walk or some moderate exercise—when you split it up, 25 minutes of exercise becomes easy to do.

Myth 7: I'm too weak to exercise

Luckily, exercising helps to build strength and regain your independence. If you are managing an illness that leaves you tired and feeling weak, exercise is a great way to get your energy back. Remember that you can always start slow and continue to progress from there.

Key Takeaways

- Sarcopenia is a common condition among seniors that can affect quality of life. While there are no medications available for treating it at the moment, regular exercise is highly recommended.
- For fitness and wellness, nutrition and exercise go hand-in-hand to increase their health benefits.
- Remember that exercising is good for all ages, and you shouldn't place any limits on yourself and your abilities. There are many different exercises to choose from, and you can start with those that are perfect for your body and comfort level.
- Adding exercise to your routine as a senior may be a bit difficult—especially when you haven't done it in a long time—but it's not impossible and far easier than you think.

Starting Strong

- Take a note or small piece of paper and list the misconceptions or myths that have prevented you from exercising.
- On the back of the note, write down whether or not your perception of exercising has changed, how it has changed, and your plan moving forward.

CHAPTER 3:

SETTING ACHIEVABLE GOALS

As humans, having and smashing goals is part of our everyday lives. Goals are set yearly by families, businesses, and individuals, and this provides direction, a clear focus, and clarifies importance.

Regardless of what you seek to achieve, setting achievable goals makes it quite a bit easier. For instance, you cannot be earning thirty thousand dollars annually and wanting to achieve a higher amount the following year without the proper planning in regard to adding a skill to earn more money, in order to get a job with more pay than you earned the previous year.

Likewise, staying fit requires achievable goals. No gym instructor would tell you to start at the pace of a veteran. It starts with the simplest workouts and evolves into something more as you get stronger.

Setting achievable goals aids in self-development. It helps you improve gradually till you are satisfied with your growth. It gives you the feeling that your fitness journey has a sense of direction. However, you should know that setting achievable goals is time-consuming, and without commitment to them, the chances of not seeing your plans through to the end are high.

After setting goals for yourself, it is necessary to create a step-by-step guide to being successful. This is where SMART GOALS come to play.

What Is A SMART Goal?

The term SMART goal is a guide to setting achievable goals. It is an acronym that stands for:

S means Specific

M means Measurable

A means Achievable

R means Realistic

T means Timely

Smart goals integrate these criteria to ensure that all your efforts are focused on achieving your fitness goals. It also reduces the chances of failure. These criteria will be elaborated on below.

Specific Goals

When your goal is specific, the chances that you'll achieve it become higher. It gives you a greater chance of success against generalized goals. For your goal to pass as being specific, it needs to pass the WH questions test. You'll need to answer the following questions:

- What exactly am I hoping to achieve?
- What motivates me to achieve this goal?
- Where should this goal be achieved?
- When should I set a timeline for accomplishing this objective?

- Who is involved in achieving this objective?

Once you've given answers to these questions, goals become specific and achievable. Here are some examples that will give you an insight into making your goals specific.

Example:

- General Goal: I want to hit the gym and keep fit.
- Specific Goal: I'm getting registered at the gym close to my house and I will be working out three days weekly because I want to lose weight, and good health is essential. I will check my progress monthly.

OR

- Every morning by 10am, I'm going to go to the living room/front porch and workout for 15 minutes. I'm going to check my progress bi-weekly.

The difference between general and specific goals is the fact that the specific goal involves detailed analysis of what you want to achieve and the steps it involves.

When a goal is specific, it becomes clear what you want to achieve. Your focus becomes narrow and fixed, getting a better understanding of the goal and how to achieve it.

Measurable Goals

For a goal to be smart, it must include a yardstick for checking progress. When this is absent, checking progress becomes frustrating and when the determination of your goal's progress is hard, keeping track and knowing when you've achieved your goal becomes difficult. But how do you measure your goals? You need to ask these questions and answer them yourself.

- How much?

- What are the signs that will inform me that I've reached my goal?
- What are my progress signs?

Let's look at an example used when we talked about specific goals:

I'm getting registered at the gym close to my house and I will be working out three days a week because I want to lose weight and good health is essential. I will check my progress monthly. Weekly, I will be losing two pounds of body fat.

The weekly checks ensure that you can measure your goals, check your progress, and keep you on the right track.

Achievable Goals

People make the mistake of setting goals that aren't easily achievable. Let's look at a quick example. **I want to run three kilometers non-stop by the end of the week (when you cannot run for 500 meters without stopping and you haven't built the endurance for three kilometers.)**

For a goal to be SMART, it must pass the test of being achievable and feasible. With this, it becomes easier to sort out ways to achieve your goal and work in line with it. The best way to make your goal achievable is to spread it over a period of time. This will challenge you, and you'll be committed to achieving it. Also, it is important to define the goal to boost achievability. Understanding whether or not your goals are achievable can be known by answering these questions:

- Who has done this before, if any, and how did they go about it?
- With my resources, can I achieve this goal? Otherwise, what is missing?

Once you can answer these questions, and your answers are positive, then your goals have passed the achievable test. But, where your answers are negative, then you need to work on making it right, getting the correct resources, and seeking help from people who have successfully achieved your goal.

Realistic Goals

For a goal to be smart, it must be realistic. That is, with the time and resources available to you, your goal should be realistically achievable. It is important to note that the more you believe that a goal can be achieved or accomplished, the more likely it is to pass the realistic test.

However, finding out whether or not your goal is realistic can be done by asking the following questions and answering them yourself:

- With the resources and time at my disposal, is this goal achievable?
- Can I be committed to accomplishing this goal?
- Does this goal fit within my capabilities, and can I realistically achieve it?
- Can I reach it despite my existing health issues (if any)?

When you can answer these questions positively, your goal has passed the realistic test.

Timely Goals

People make mistakes when setting goals that are not time-bound.

Every goal must be timely to ensure that it is achievable. It must have both a start date and a finish date. Simply put, it must be time-bound. The presence of time creates urgency, and it would serve as an extra rationale to accomplish the goal. Lack of a time-bound goal makes you less motivated about it. Here are some questions to determine whether or not your goal is time-bound:

- When do I want to accomplish my goal?
- When is the deadline for achieving this goal?

Let's look at an example of a timely goal, using the example we have been building upon.

Example: I'm getting registered at the gym close to my house and I will be working out three days weekly because I want to lose weight, and good health is essential. I will check my progress monthly. **Weekly**, I will be losing two pounds of body fat. My goal will be realized if, at the end of the **month**, I've lost seven pounds.

Take note of the bolded letters in this example. This goal has both weekly and monthly time bounds, and this is good because it gives extra motivation to achieve the goal. It is registered in your subconscious mind that you need to lose two pounds weekly, and seven pounds by the end of the month. This creates urgency and boosts the chances that you will achieve this goal.

Importance of SMART Goals

Now that you have an understanding of SMART goals and what each letter stands for. However, what is the importance of this framework? Why is it important for you to make SMART goals as an individual?

- **It makes you focused and offers clarity for goal achievements**

With SMART goals, you are clear about what you want to do and how you want to do it. They breed focus and ensure that you don't leave a goal unfinished. They offer clarity from start to finish because your goal is specific. You aren't building a house and thinking about another house at the same time.

Basically, SMART goals teach you to take things one at a time and give them your all. This boosts chances of success rather than becoming a jack of all trades, attempting a lot at once and failing to achieve any at the end.

- **SMART Goals ensure that you are keen to every detail necessary to accomplish your goal**

One good thing about SMART goals is the fact that nothing regarding your goal will be overlooked. There is nothing like a particular plan that is primary or secondary in achieving your goal, examining all details that may be of great help, or that may serve as hindrances to the success of your goal.

Every step to achieving your goals should be examined over and over again. Are they time-bound? Are they attainable? Specific? Realistic? These questions will be answered in line with every detail necessary to make your goals successful and in the end, you'll be easily committed, and it will be effortless to remain unflinching even when there are challenges.

- **It builds mental preparation**

SMART goals build mental preparation for the incoming tasks and sacrifices. You become mentally aware of what you need to do and how to go about it. For instance, if your goal is weight loss, your mental preparation would most definitely cause you to reduce the calories you consume daily, even before you hit the gym. Likewise, a person who has a goal to save a particular amount would most likely cut down on spending too much before they start saving.

Also, being mentally prepared helps to regulate your actions. It gives you insight into what needs to be done and allows you to become focused, and conscious of situations that may take your attention away from the goal at hand.

This mental preparation only happens when the goal passes the SMART test. This means it has been given a good amount of thought, and you are mentally prepared for what lies ahead. Lastly, mental preparation boosts your commitment to achieving the goal.

Mistakes to Avoid When Making SMART Goals

After equipping yourself with a SMART goal, some mistakes may hamper your actions in achieving your goals.

- **Being too vague**

Just like the one the SMART Framework provides, being specific is better than being vague. Some people tend to be partially specific, and this isn't good. For instance, **I want to finish three books in three months. I'll check my progress monthly**.

While this seems like a SMART goal, it is also vague and not as specific as it should have been because there is no indication of the genre, the type of books you're going to read, or if you'll be interested enough to see it through to the end.

Let's write this example in a more specific way. **I want to read three self-help books in three months. I'll read each book for a month, and check my progress at the end of each month in a little note or journal entry**.

This example is more specific and not vague, making it clear to execute, increasing your chances of being successful.

- **Failing to understand the place of challenges can affect our progress**

Facing challenges and obstacles in your fitness journey is a given, but that doesn't make them exciting. These challenges can tamper with your motivation and cause you to believe that you can't make the changes you want to see in your journey to health. If you allow them to overwhelm you, you might end up giving up or going through the process half-heartedly.

But what you should understand about these challenges is that they give you a better understanding of yourself, and vital information which will aid you in fine-tuning your strategies to achieve your fitness goals.

- **Making no plans for future problems**

Regardless of whether or not your strategy on your goals will work, it is essential to prepare ahead. If there is a possibility that your work schedule or health issues will prevent you from having enough time to exercise, think about a time that will work for you and do it.

How to Track Your Progress

How do you know you are getting it right? How do you know how well you've done? Tracking your goal progress ensures that you remain focused, and here are some steps to effectively track your goal progress:

- **Make a list**

One of the first ways to keep track of your progress is by making a list of all your goals. Get a paper and pen. Write down those goals including the time duration and every other detail. Remember, be specific.

Once you have written your goals down this takes a big chunk out of your issues, as you don't need to start recollecting the exact number of these goals.

This list should be pasted in an area of your house where you visit a couple of times daily, or it could be in your journal or diary where you get to see it daily. The latter is advisable if your line of work requires you to travel frequently.

- **Break it up using little tasks**

Your goal will always have a result. For instance, the goal in the gym example we have dwelled upon in this chapter is losing body fat and maintaining good health. But, how do you know you are on the right track? This can be done using small, easily achievable tasks. Break down your goal into little tasks.

For example, before going to the gym, one of your little tasks could be light jogging before hitting the gym to do exercises that support the loss of body fat. Also, it is important to note that breaking goals into smaller tasks makes the final goal less overwhelming, giving you a confidence boost upon its achievement.

- **Reward yourself when you hit a milestone**

Give yourself a treat when you reach a milestone with weights, if you go beyond your usual daily squats, or you jog more miles than ever before. This builds motivation, and you are effectively tracking your progress.

However, celebrating your success shouldn't undermine your progress. Reward yourself in a way that is satisfying, without negating all the work you've put in. For instance, you may want to celebrate your progress by having some snacks, but remember not to go overboard with it.

- **Review progress frequently**

Lastly, you need to monitor progress by reviewing your activities weekly. For instance, if you seek to lose two pounds of body fat per week, and at the end of the week you find out that you only lost 1.6 pounds, you'll be able to ask questions as to what went wrong and how to correct it. Also, it ensures that you won't be waiting too long to determine your level of progress, which boosts commitment.

How To Stay Motivated When Achieving Your Goal

Staying motivated has always been a major problem faced by individuals attempting to pursue a goal. Here are some tips to ensure that you stay true to your goal from start to finish.

- Assess the goals you set and how well you have progressed in achieving them on a regular basis.
- Understand that growth is a terrific incentive in itself, and it enhances your self-esteem.
- Never stop setting new objectives for yourself. Always give thoughts on what you seek to accomplish in the coming week, month, and year. To avoid feeling overwhelmed, focus on one goal at a time.
- Maintain the momentum. Most individuals need about three months before mastering a new habit. So, you don't have to force yourself to learn it in under a month. Continuing with your routine and being committed makes your actions into a habit in no time.
- Seek a support group. Joining a support group, including the use of social media platforms with groups

for the kind of goal you are after, is one of the easiest ways of finding a mentor that shares similar beliefs.

Having a support group or partner will provide you with accountability and give you someone to rely on because they are going through the same thing as you.

Also, when looking for a support group, surround yourself with people who dwell on the positives rather than the negatives. This will improve your self-talk and limit the number of times you feel like quitting. Having these people around also reduces feelings of depression.

- Exercise even when you don't feel like it. There are days when you won't have enough motivation to get you out of bed; on those days, discipline matters more than anything.

While you should always have rest days and take your health into consideration when exercising, it is important that you don't forget why you're on this journey and ensure that you take the needed steps to see positive results.

Key Takeaways

- The term SMART goal is a guide to setting achievable goals.
- It is important in keeping you focused and clear on what you want to achieve, building mental preparation for what lies ahead, and ensuring that you are abreast of every detail needed in achieving your goal.
- Avoid mistakes like being too vague, fear of failing, and failing to make plans for future problems. These mistakes limit the number of people who eventually achieve their goals.

- Make a goals list, break them up into little tasks, access your progress frequently, and reward yourself for work done. This makes achieving your goals easier.
- Staying motivated is hard, but by accessing your goals, exercising, making positive friends, getting a mentor, etc., you can remain unflinching in the course of achieving them.

Starting Strong

Now you have read all I've written about setting achievable goals. It is now time to act on what you've read.

- Review your goals. Do they pass the SMART test? If not, fine-tune those goals right now.
- List out your goals and break them down into little reasonable tasks, then make plans to reward yourself for a job well done.
- Plan ahead for problems that may arise, give them critical thought, and provide solutions.

CHAPTER 4:

BREAKING THROUGH THE PLATEAU

Imagine this. You started exercising regularly, and even though there were days when you had to dig deep to finish the program, you kept pushing and never gave up. After a few weeks or months, your body started showing the results of all that hard work. You lost some of the excess weight you had, and you could do things you love without feeling worn out easily. You feel happier and better every day, and your health is starting to change for the better.

After a few more months of sticking to the same routine and diet plan, those gains stop coming. Whenever you check yourself, you discover that you are no longer losing weight, gaining endurance, and generally becoming stronger. What's happening to your body? The answer is simple: you've reached a fitness plateau.

When we see obvious results or progress from sticking to our fitness routine, it gives us that extra motivation that keeps us pushing forward because we want to look in the mirror, or go for our next doctor's appointment, and see more of those results.

Seeing progress gives you a sense of satisfaction and accomplishment, especially when you struggled with exercise in the beginning, because it is a sign of how far you've come, the journey that remains, and shows you that everything you want regarding your health is well within your reach. But when these results stop coming despite consistency, it can be a bit frustrating, and some might even decide to give up on exercising rather than discovering what's happening and how to change it. So, what is a fitness plateau?

Fitness plateaus happen when your progress has stalled, despite consistently following your fitness plan. In essence, your body doesn't respond to your fitness routine like it used to; you experience a sudden stop in your weight loss or feel weaker because your body is not making any more progress with your muscle strength. Fitness plateaus are a testament to your body's wonderful ability to adapt to stress, and change when repeatedly exposed to the same training. It is not something to be ashamed of—quite the contrary—because it shows that you have been consistent in your fitness journey and your body is ready to go to the next stage. If you are happy with your progress, a fitness plateau is a good place to be, as it only becomes frustrating if you believe that there is still work to be done.

Apart from your body adapting to these changes, there are other reasons why you may have reached a fitness plateau or stopped seeing progress:

- You may not have been consistent with your fitness routine. Sometimes, you may not be too conscious of what you eat and the amount of effort you put into your workouts. If you still eat ultra-processed or other high-calorie foods with little to no nutritional value, you may not see as much progress as you would like over time.

Also, if you've been skipping some parts of your workouts or rarely complete them, your progress may stall.

- You are not getting enough rest. It is important to get about seven to eight hours of quality sleep to start your day on a high note, but there are several factors that can affect your ability to enjoy a good night's rest, such as insomnia and sleep apnea.

  Not getting enough sleep puts your body under a lot of pressure, and gives it less time to recover from the day's stress or enjoy the impact of exercising, because it is working overtime to avoid breaking down. If you have a sporadic sleeping pattern and haven't seen any progress from your fitness routine, you may want to consider getting more sleep to give your body a chance to recover and heal.

- You didn't set realistic goals. We will always look for the quickest way to get what we want, and we may set goals that do not adequately represent where we are health-wise, and what it would take to get to where we want to be. So, when your progress isn't meeting those expectations, it may seem like you've plateaued even when you haven't.

- You reduced your total daily activity. In the previous chapter, we talked about NEAT and how the activities under this category are crucial for your overall health. However, it is easy to want to skip those activities when you exercise regularly. For example, instead of going out to buy groceries like you used to, you may decide to have them delivered because you believe that your daily fitness requirements have been met through your workout. When you consciously or unconsciously limit your daily activities, it can affect your progress.

So, if you've been doing everything right by remaining consistent with your fitness routine and giving your body enough time to recover but still see no visible progress, you may have hit a plateau.

There are a few signs to look out for if you aren't sure whether or not you have reached a fitness plateau. These indicators are:

- It starts to feel easy: when you begin a fitness routine for the first time, the first few weeks of starting your new routine can feel exhilarating and challenging because your body is pushing its current limits, but after six months or more of repeating that same routine, it starts to feel normal. When it gets to a point where you can complete your workout routine with minimal effort, and you no longer see any progress, you have reached a fitness plateau.
- You are not motivated or focused on doing the workouts. Sometimes, you may not be motivated to workout due to overtraining, high stress levels, or not giving your body enough time to recover, but a lack of motivation or focus can be another way of knowing if you've reached a plateau. We all enjoy having some form of challenge when exercising because it keeps us focused on the task at hand. Therefore, if it ever gets to a point where you go through your routine without feeling any form of satisfaction from it, that means it's time to move to the next level.

Ways to Break Through Your Plateau

When you hit a fitness plateau, there are ways you can tackle the issue and start seeing some progress again. However, remember that there is no need to do this if you are happy with where you are and just want to maintain those results.

To break through your plateau, you can:

Embrace rest

When you start seeing some results or want to meet your fitness goals faster, it is easy to fall into the habit of overtraining. Asking too much of your body can make it exhausted and stall any progress you've made.

Taking enough time to rest is just as important as exercising, because your body needs enough time to recover and improve its capabilities. Depending on your fitness level and health conditions, take a day or two to rest and not worry about working out or anything else. By the time you get back up, you'll have enough energy to keep going and break through your fitness plateau.

Increase the intensity

When you start to feel bored or unmotivated with your routine, it may be time to increase its intensity. For instance, you can increase the weights you carry by 1kg or more depending on your ability and see if that tasks your body to do more. If you've been doing moderate-intensity exercises for 15-20 minutes you can increase the time you spend by five minutes or try some exercises with more intensity.

Going at a slower pace by choosing lighter exercises can also help when you've been doing more high-intensity exercises.

Before you make any changes to your routine, talk to your doctor or physician for safety purposes. Also, when increasing the intensity of your workouts, it's advisable not to change everything at once or take it too high; rather make small incremental changes in exercise intensity or duration.

Make a few small changes here and there, increasing the intensity little by little until you get to that point where your exercises can provide enough challenge without being painful or putting you in harm's way.

Try something new

Variety is the spice of life, and that certainly holds true when it comes to breaking through a fitness plateau. When you do the same routine every day, it will get repetitive, and even though your body will be enjoying the benefits of exercise, there will be little to no physical progress.

If you've been doing more aerobics or cardio exercises than strength training, you can make strength training your focus for a while and see what it does for you. Plus, you can remove one or two exercises from your routine and replace them with something completely different.

Another way to vary your workout is to change the order in which you do those exercises. For example, you can change the order by making the 4th and 5th exercises in your routine to be the first exercises performed and making the exercises you typically do first as the last set.

When that doesn't work, changing your entire routine can be a good way to go. Look for exercises you've never done before, or those you rarely do, and try them out. Having a complete change can help reset your metabolism and give you visible progress.

Check your nutrition

Sometimes, what you need to break through your plateau is a change in diet and not necessarily your workouts. Your body needs proper nutrition to function properly, and poor nutrition can stall your progress no matter how much effort you put into exercising.

It is crucial that you meet your daily caloric requirements in order to get all the essential nutrients. Where you need to maintain muscle mass, increase your intake of protein and carbohydrates. If you are not sure about what to do, speak to your nutritionist or doctor regarding the changes to your diet, taking any preexisting health conditions into consideration.

Get a partner

Working out is always better when you have someone doing it with you. If inconsistency has stalled your progress, having a partner can bring that extra motivation and change to keep going.

You can change your environment or go to places in your home where you haven't worked out before. In good weather, occasionally working out in your garden or local park can have a huge impact in how you exercise. Having a partner is also a great way to track your progress and keep you accountable.

Decrease your workouts

When your body still finds it difficult to recover after decreasing the intensity of your workouts, one way to break through your plateau could be to reduce your training for about a week or more.

If you work out five to six days a week, take it down to four days, giving your body extra time to recover. You can always keep moving by continuing your daily activities or doing some light stretching and yoga exercises to help your body repair and heal.

Focus on your mindset

It may not seem important, but your mindset towards plateaus can affect your ability to push through them. If you let the feeling of frustration get to you, it is easy to undo all the progress you've made and head back to square one. But if you take the time to acknowledge your frustration, focus on why you are feeling unmotivated, or what is preventing you from resting properly, you can find effective solutions to those problems.

Take some minutes to meditate and practice mindfulness to regain control over your thoughts and keep yourself relaxed despite the stall in your progress.

Tracking your progress can help

You can't know for certain if you've hit a plateau when you are not tracking your progress in any way. To track your progress, you can take pictures of yourself in the same sportswear every two weeks to see visible results, and you can track your workouts and meals in a journal. There are fitness platforms like myfitnesspal that make tracking your progress easier and more enjoyable.

By tracking your progress, you can get a better idea of what caused your plateau, and what you can do differently to see a change.

Key Takeaways

- At some point in your fitness journey, you are going to experience a fitness plateau, and how you deal with it can make or break your journey.
- Sometimes, a stall in your progress can be caused by stress and lack of rest, which is why you should always get enough quality sleep.
- To get through a plateau, you should consider changing your workout routine, diet plan, and making general changes in your lifestyle to see results.

Starting Strong

- Have you ever experienced a fitness plateau before, maybe when you were younger, or at this stage of your life? Try to remember how it made you feel, and what you did to overcome it.
- Note some factors in your life that you think can stall your progress.

CHAPTER 5:
GETTING STARTED

In 2019, Nicholas Rizzo, a former powerlifter, biologist, and fitness research director at RunRepeat, believed that exercising is crucial for adults as they age. Using his knowledge of fitness and exercise he helped his father, who was in his early 60s, to lose 25 pounds and prevent becoming pre-diabetic. Getting his father to this stage didn't happen all at once. Rizzo started by encouraging his father to make small changes to his daily routine—these changes, along with a healthy diet, got Rizzo's father into the best shape of his life.

You already know that exercising regularly as you age keeps you active and reduces the risk of health issues, but the challenge lies in getting started. Whether you're someone who exercised when you were younger, or a person who never exercised before but kept fit due to a busy lifestyle, it's time to get serious with your fitness by making exercise an essential part of your daily routine. In this chapter, we'll be discussing some practical steps that will help you get started on the right foot and lead to a fantastic experience.

What to Know About Exercising as a Senior

If you were not as active as you would have liked throughout adulthood, you can't get into the habit of exercising regularly without ticking a few boxes first. Before starting your fitness journey, here are some things you should know.

1. **Talk to your doctor first:** You must talk to your doctor before starting any exercise program. Increasing your physical activity may affect the prescription and dosage of your medications. Your doctor may have to restrict you from doing some exercises at the beginning due to underlying health conditions.

It is necessary to talk to your doctor if:

- **You haven't been active for a while:** You may have cardiac complications or an increased risk of heart attack if you jump right in after being inactive for a long period of time. Your internal organs and joints will also need to be checked before exercising to reduce the risk of injuries.
- **You have arthritis:** Increased motion is a big help for people with arthritis because it strengthens the muscles surrounding the joints, but not all exercises can be performed if you are dealing with painful joints. So, you may need to consider different options, and choose those that will have less impact on your joints while pushing you towards your fitness goals. Your doctor or trainer can help determine the best exercises for you.
- **You've gone for surgery:** Doing strenuous exercises right after surgery puts a lot of pressure on your body, affecting its healing process. Pushing yourself too hard or getting into an exercise routine too soon after surgery can lead to complications such as infection,

fluid buildup, swelling, wound separation, and bruising.

After giving your body some time to heal, your doctor may recommend basic physical therapy and low-impact exercises to get you moving again, in order to reduce the risk of complications and aid in your healing process. The intensity of the activities will gradually increase until your body is fully healed.

- **You've recently experienced a heart attack:** Exercising after a heart attack helps to reduce the possibility of having other heart complications, but you need to talk to your doctor about what type of exercises to do to recuperate faster, and determine the best time to start exercising again. Also, depending on the severity of the attack and the possibility of exercise increasing cardiac output, the doctor may be required to change your medications or dosages to suit your present health needs.

- **You have high blood pressure:** Being physically active is great for people with high blood pressure, but it may increase it, especially when you haven't been physically active. Ask your doctor about any restrictions that may apply, and the types of exercises you should focus on in order to reduce the risk of injuries, to ensure you get all the benefits of exercising.

- **You have diabetes:** Regular exercise affects how your body responds to insulin and can change your blood sugar levels. For instance, your blood sugar levels may drop after exercising, and pose health risks if it happens continuously.

  Having a doctor guide you when exercising with Type I or Type II diabetes, or issues with blood sugar, provides that extra level of safety. You know what to look out for before and after exercising, and the steps to ensure that you are always healthy. For example, your doctor may advise that you check your blood sugar levels before and after exercising or have a snack after working out if your blood sugar level drops.

2. **Go slow but steady:** Going full speed ahead will only result in injury and setbacks and may cause you to stop working out altogether. Start with warmup exercises to get your body moving, and end every exercise session with a cooldown session. Also, get comfortable with low-intensity exercises, focusing on correct posture before increasing the intensity—once you've gotten comfortable with your form, you can take it up a notch. Also, pay attention to your surroundings for anything that can injure you, especially when exercising outside.

3. **Have a way to measure your progress:** tracking your progress is an excellent way to stay motivated, especially in the beginning, when you're not yet seeing visible results. Tracking your process doesn't have to be complicated, and there are several ways you can do this:

- **Use a notebook or journal:** make detailed notes about your workouts, so you can include the results you want to see, including the time frames for them.
- **Take body measurements:** use a measuring tape to take accurate measurements of your waist, arms, chest, hips, and other areas where you want to see progress. Take new measurements weekly or bi-weekly to see if you are making progress.
- **Take progress pictures after working out:** pictures don't lie and are one of the best ways to track chang-

es. When possible, take after workout photos (weekly or bi-weekly) in the same gym wear.

- **Get a scale:** using a scale to track your progress is great if your primary goal is weight loss, but it doesn't give a clear picture of what is going on inside your body. Because muscle weighs more than fat, your weight may remain the same on the scale, or you may not see much of a change in your outward appearance, even when your body fat percentage is reduced. When using a body weight scale, try to combine it with other methods of tracking your progress.

- **Use a pedometer or fitness watch to track your workouts:** this is an automatic way to keep up with your progress. As long as you're wearing the fitness watch and have the apps installed on your phone, your results can be tracked to give you an accurate overview of how much effort you've put into your fitness, including the resulting changes.

4. **Choose different exercises but make sure they are suitable for you:** the best part about starting your fitness journey is that there are a variety of exercises and workout programs to choose from. Include a mix of aerobics, strength training, balance, and stretching exercises, all with the right intensity to push you towards your goals. If you find it difficult to do a specific fitness program, remember that it was made to fit you, and not the other way around. Put it aside, start with something easier, and go back to it when you can handle the program.

5. **Always remain hydrated:** committing to regular exercise means you must focus on eating well-balanced meals with just enough calories to fuel your body. Also, always have a water bottle with you and make

sure to drink water before, during, and after workouts, even when you don't feel thirsty.

Exercising regularly for the first time can seem a bit daunting but implementing these tips can make it easier and encourage you to keep pushing forward.

Equipment Needed for Exercising

Although everyone has different preferences for exercise, there is no doubt that having the right workout equipment can go a long way in your fitness journey. These tools are used to:

1. **Give you better control:** proper workout equipment can control the way your body moves and regulate the amount of pressure placed on the body. This prevents your body from getting overworked and tired.

2. **Faster Results:** using the right workout equipment can give you quicker results and a more toned body. For instance, using hand weights will strengthen your muscles better than regular unweighted exercises, and having a treadmill or exercise bike in your home is an excellent way to incorporate some cardio into your lifestyle, boosting your energy levels and stamina.

3. **Increases performance and time efficiency:** different equipment allows you to target various body parts and make the most out of your schedule. These workout tools also increase how much effort you can put into your fitness routine within a limited time frame.

You can have simple tools in your home to make exercising enjoyable and effective.

These tools are:

Good shoes

When exercising, shoes do more than cover your feet. They support the ankles, cushion the pressure exerted on your feet when exercising, and prevent injury. It is necessary to have shoes that are comfortable, with a firm heel and flexibility to aid movement. Therefore, before settling on any athletic shoes, test them by walking around in them or using the in-store treadmill if there is one.

Yoga mat

A yoga mat provides a soft surface upon which to do low-impact exercises that require you to lie on your back or use your feet and knees. It's great for stretching exercises like Pilates and yoga that tone your body, strengthen your core, and improve balance.

Stability Balls

Stability balls or exercise balls are great for building endurance, strength, and balance. To prove this, a study in 2014 noted that older adults who used exercise balls five days a week for two months saw improvement in their muscle activity (Kim et al., 2014).

They come in different sizes and colors that you can choose from depending on your preference. In addition, test the stability ball by sitting on it before you take it home to ensure that you are comfortable with it.

Weights

For strength training and maintaining your muscle mass, you may want to include weights in your home gym. You can get some dumbbells, barbells, and wrist weights in different sizes and switch to heavier weights as you get stronger. If you don't want to use weights, you can get resistance bands instead, because they are easier to handle and help with strength training.

Jump Rope

Using a jump rope is a way to include a full body workout into your lifestyle, and it is great for seniors with joint pain because it doesn't put a lot of pressure on the joints such as with running.

Jumping rope also increases your agility, strength, and bone mineral density, which in turn reduces the development of osteoporosis.

Resistance Bands

If you don't want to use weights, you can try resistance bands which are available in different strengths (resistances) instead.

Resistance bands have gained in popularity recently because they are easier to handle than weights, and they help with strength training.

Medicine Balls

You already know about using dumbbells or weights for strength training, and to add a bit of variation to your workout, but medicine balls can also do the work. They aid dynamic movement and support the rehabilitation of muscle groups after having surgery or an injury. Plus, when using medicine balls, your muscles are more engaged, which helps to improve your flexibility and movement.

When used for strength training, medicine balls add an extra level of intensity, especially when doing exercises like squats and lunges.

Stationary Bicycle

If you enjoyed riding bicycles when you were younger, then having a stationary bike will be a welcome addition. With this type of exercise bicycle, you don't have to worry about losing your balance, and you can continue to track your progress, as newer models often come with mobile apps for such purposes.

Elliptical Machine

An elliptical machine will help to include cardio exercise into your fitness routine. It puts less pressure on your knees, hips, and joints than running and other high-intensity cardio exercises, and is a fun way to burn calories quickly.

With this machine, you can switch between high-intensity cardio workouts and medium-intensity exercises, which helps if you're trying to improve your balance or remain fit after an injury.

Treadmill

Having a treadmill in your home helps prevent loss of muscle mass and makes cardio a part of your lifestyle. The good news is you can use it irrespective of how the weather is outside, and set it to whatever intensity you want. Customize the impact, incline, and intensity to suit your comfort level while providing some challenge. You can keep changing the settings to suit your needs as you progress.

Substitutes for Some Workout Equipment

What if you're unable to go to the gym, or you already have some of the aforementioned equipment at home? While the equipment does help, not having it around you doesn't mean you can't work out effectively and see results. Also, there are simple household items that can serve as workout equipment when you feel the need to add something extra to your fitness routine. Some of these items are:

- **Water bottles:** these can serve as an alternative to light hand weights. Look for bottles you can hold comfortably and fill them with water. However, when using them to exercise, you may have to do longer repetitions (reps) to feel the same impact as a hand weight.
- **Chairs:** dips help to tone your triceps and chest, and you can usually find dip stands in gyms or workout rooms for this purpose; a chair can be a suitable alternative to a dip stand. Get a chair behind you when doing dips and do the movement properly by exerting the right pressure when performing the exercise. For squats, using a chair or couch provides extra support and enables you to do the exercise properly.
- **Water jug:** kettlebells are great for improving flexibility, balance, core power, coordination, and strength, while toning your muscles; using a water jug can have the same effect. Get a jug with a tight cover to prevent the water from spilling out—it should have a strong handle that won't break when swinging it. You can start with a small to medium water jug as a beginner, and gradually move to a bigger one as you get stronger.
- **Basketball or football to replace medicine balls:** just like a medicine ball, using a basketball or football can strengthen your mind-muscle connection, and improve your balance and coordination. When doing exercises like Russian Twists, using a medicine ball or football/ basketball can work on your core and obliques.
- **Pillows:** placing them close to your lower back can provide a bit of incline similar to what you would get from a workout bench for exercises like crunches or bench presses.

- **Small bag of rice:** this can be an alternative to lighter dumbbells for exercises such as bench presses, squats, overhead extensions, and deadlifts.

These alternatives can help save some money as you meet your fitness goals, but safety should always come first when using them. Try them out first to see if you are comfortable with them. Talk to your trainer or doctor about how you can use these items safely. If that is not an option, there are YouTube channels available that can provide you with that type of much-needed information.

Key Takeaways

- You do not require expensive pieces of equipment to get started. Inexpensive alternatives are often available, and there are many bodyweight exercises which do not require any equipment.
- Workout equipment, from a simple yoga mat or medicine ball through to stationary bikes, are great for toning your body and achieving better results.
- You don't have to go to the gym if you can create a workout area at home. You only need a few pieces of equipment, and you're good to go.
- Safety always comes first when using exercise equipment, or any of their alternatives.

Starting Strong

- Depending on your budget, make a list of some exercise equipment that you would like to have at home.
- If that's not an option, consider the alternatives you have lying around your home, and determine how they can be put to good use.

CHAPTER 6:

STRETCHING EXERCISES

In 2014, a study was done using seniors between the ages of 67-80 to examine the effects of stretching on muscle strength and flexibility. They were asked to participate in a static stretching program for about a year, and the exercises were to be done five times a week. After a year, tests were done on the participants, and the results showed that their flexibility went up by 31%, and muscle strength showed an increase of a 10-17% (Inami, 2014).

One of the effects of the physiological changes that happen when you age is a decrease in musculoskeletal flexibility. Your muscles become stiff, and daily activities become difficult to perform. By now, you are probably aware of the importance of including cardio, strength, and resistance training exercises in your lifestyle, but one area that is sometimes neglected and does not receive as much attention as it deserves is stretching.

Stretching is a type of physical activity whereby a specific muscle is stretched or flexed to tone the muscle and make it more elastic or flexible. There are many reasons why you should include stretching exercises in your fitness regimen:

- **It improves flexibility:** this is one of the key benefits of regular stretching. As you age, your muscles become shorter, tighter, and stiff, but stretching exercises or yoga can help with that. Stretching makes your muscles loose and limber, making everyday activities like getting out of bed, tying your shoes, and reaching for objects easier.

- **Increases blood circulation:** stretching encourages blood flow to your muscles and joints. This helps your muscles recover quickly after a workout and reduces muscle soreness. Plus, stretching can aid in the healing process of an existing injury, and reduce the risk of muscle strain and back pain.
- **Increases your range of motion:** stretching increases your range of motion by supporting your joints, ligaments, and tendons. Having an increased range of motion makes you agile and prevents you from sustaining injuries due to imbalance.
- **It improves your mood:** every day, we go through events that increase our stress levels and make it difficult for us to relax. When that stress builds, it may have a negative effect on our sleeping patterns and eating habits by causing unintentional weight loss or gain. When you are stressed, you get tired easily, and your body becomes open to both physical and emotional health issues such as depression, heart problems, digestive issues, depression, and sometimes a weakened immune system. However, something as simple as stretching can change all that.

In 1993, a study published by the Department of Experimental Psychology at Oxford University determined that a simple 30-minute program combining both yoga and breathing exercises had a strong effect on both mental and physical energy, including a noted improvement in mood (Wood, 1993). Combined with the endorphins released when you work out, and controlled breathing, stretching exercises can put your body in a calm and relaxed state.

- **Helps in managing chronic health conditions:** when combined with exercise, stretching can reduce the risk of some chronic diseases like insomnia, anxiety, high blood pressure, and heart disease. They may also have therapeutic effects beneficial to your health.

- **Improves your posture:** having loose and flexible muscles prevents muscle imbalance, which is one of the common causes of poor posture. When you stretch, your core muscles are strengthened, supporting your body, and giving you the ability to stand straight and tall.

Stretching occasionally isn't going to automatically make you flexible or agile—it is going to take time and commitment before seeing any results. In addition, it is crucial to follow safety protocols and proper stretching techniques to remain safe and reap all the benefits of regular stretching. This is why we are going to be discussing some safety protocols and tips that will help you make the most out of these exercises.

Safety Protocols and Tips for Proper Stretching

Before we get into the tips and protocols, it is necessary to discuss the two main types of stretches to prevent injuries and improve your performance. These types of are:

- **Static Stretching**

These exercises are usually done in one position or in a stationary mode. Here each muscle is stretched to its limit, and it is recommended that you do this type of stretching after a workout session when your muscles are already warm, because they may have a negative effect on your performance if done as warm up exercises.

For instance, a study that examined the effects of static stretching on sprint performance in college athletes noted a 3% decrease in performance when it was done before running (Winchester et al., 2008). Some exercises that fall under this category are the quadriceps stretch, butterfly stretch, figure-four stretch, and hamstring stretch.

- **Dynamic Stretching**

This type of stretching requires active-controlled movement and can be done as warm up exercises to prepare your body for a workout session, because they gradually reduce stiffness and increase your muscle temperature. Some exercises that fall under this category include torso twists, arm circles, high knees, high kicks, and leg swings. Also, stretching exercises done as a warmup do not have a huge impact on your flexibility.

Let's move on to the protocols and tips:

1. **Stretch regularly**

The National Institute on Aging recommends that seniors should do stretching exercises three to five times per session and should combine it with strength and endurance exercises. Similar to workout exercises, the benefits and impact of stretching cannot be truly felt until you remain consistent and make a conscious effort to make it a part of your fitness regimen.

In addition, holding the stretch for a few seconds doesn't have as much impact as you might think because it takes time for your muscles to lengthen. When doing a stretch, hold it for about 30 seconds, and have a timer beside you to keep track of the time.

2. **Stretch after a workout session for flexibility**

If your goal is flexibility, it's best not to neglect stretching after working out because your muscles are warmed up and ready to go. Another great time to stretch is before going to bed, and it doesn't have to be anything strenuous. Since your body heals and recovers while you sleep, stretching before heading in for the night lets your muscles heal in a stretched position.

3. **Focus on your breathing and try to relax**

Go as deep into the stretch as you can, but don't get to the point where it becomes painful and uncomfortable. Use that time to relax, focus on taking deep, steady breaths, and listen to some calming music if it helps you to relax.

4. **Don't bounce around**

Bouncing while stretching can cause tears in your muscles which tightens them and puts you in pain. With the exception of dynamic stretching, where you are required to make slow controlled movements, try to hold the position until the time is up before moving on to the next one.

5. **Go slowly and gently**

Slowly get into each stretching position and stop when you feel a bit of tension in the muscle without it being painful. Hold that position for about 15 seconds before going deeper into the stretch, or remain as you are if you've reached your limit.

Before getting into any stretching routine, talk to your doctor, especially if you are recovering from a health issue or have conditions such as herniated discs or osteoporosis that can limit your ability to stretch. Also, if you recently had an injury or sprained a muscle, refrain from stretching that muscle until it is properly healed.

Apart from your scheduled stretching routine, it is advisable to look for ways to stretch throughout the day to keep your muscles loose and limber. You can perform little stretches when walking around, watching television, or relaxing.

Stretching Exercises

These exercises will be divided into two categories for you to easily pick those you want to include in your fitness routine.

Warmup Exercises

Pelvic Tilts

Lie on a yoga mat, firm bed, or floor with your knee bent and your hands flat beside you.

When you exhale, tighten your abdominal muscles, and press your lower back against the floor or mat by tilting your waist backward. When you inhale, lift your lower back slightly by tilting your waist forward. Do these for 5-10 reps for the best impact.

Tips:

- Focus on doing the exercise properly, and don't forget to breathe to prevent injuries.
- Don't lift your hips or buttocks off the floor because then the exercise becomes a bridge pose rather than a pelvic tilt.
- If you are not sure about form, put a towel under your lower back. When pressing against the floor, you shouldn't be able to pull the towel from under you. When lifting your lower back, there should be just enough space to pull out the towel.

- Does it feel too easy? Then you can try a variation by lifting your feet off the floor one at a time high enough to engage your abdominal muscles, and your lower back is pressed against the floor. Then lift your lower back slightly by tilting your waist forward.

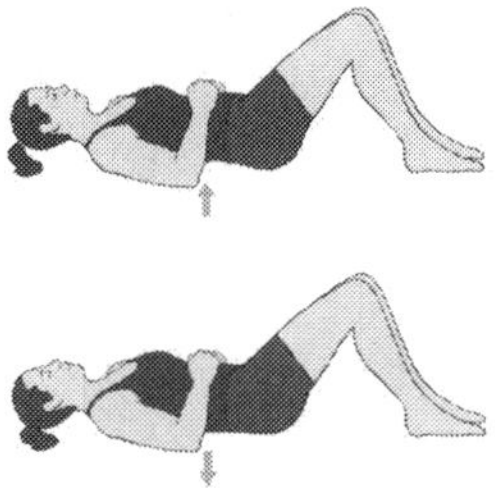

Supine Leg Stretch

Lie flat on your back using a yoga mat or a comfortable floor. Stretch one leg out on the floor and raise the other, pointing it towards the ceiling. Place your hands around your thigh to keep the leg raised as straight as possible, and give your arms a stretch as well.

Pop your ankles up and down to feel a stretch in the calf behind your knee—do this for approximately 30 seconds to a minute. Drop your leg and repeat with the other leg. If you are not flexible enough, an alteration to this stretch is to take a strap or rope, place it on the back of your foot, and use it to raise your leg until you feel a stretch. Hold the position for 30 seconds to a minute.

Remember to engage your core and keep your breath slow and steady.

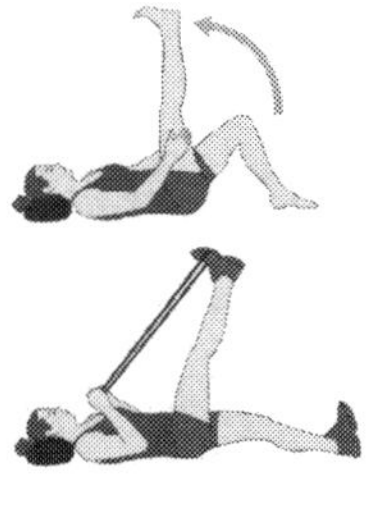

Easy Pose

Sit on a comfortable surface with your legs crossed in front of you. Place each foot beneath the opposite knee and bring it close to your torso.

Sit straight—the sit bones in your butt should be firm against the ground. Rest your hands on your knees, or anywhere that feels most comfortable and natural.

The first step is to inhale, draw your chin to your chest, and let your shoulders expand backward to feel a stretch. Hold this for a few seconds and as you exhale, then slowly return your body to its former position with your back straight. In this neutral position, rotate your shoulders to the back and front to loosen them. Also, rotate your neck clockwise for 15 seconds, and anti-clockwise for another 15 seconds, then release the position. Do this for 2-3 reps.

If it helps, sit on folded blankets, especially when you have hip and knee injuries.

Eye of the Needle Pose

Lie on a yoga mat, firm bed, or a comfortable floor with your back flat and your knees bent, with the soles of your feet firmly on the floor.

Place your right ankle right on top of your left knee with comfortable pressure. This position creates a space between the legs and an opportunity to 'thread the needle.' Use your arms to gently wrap around the hamstring of your left thigh, and gently pull the left knee towards your body while pushing the right leg back. Do this up to the point where you feel a bit of tension without pain.

Stay in this position for 30 seconds and release, but if you need a bit more challenge, place your hands above your left knee and gently bring it closer to your chest while pushing your right leg back. Repeat this with the other leg.

Tips:

- Don't force yourself to go deep into the stretch if you are not as flexible, and over time it will get easier.
- Take this as an opportunity to relax and slowly breathe in and out. When doing this stretch, your head should be lying comfortably and not feel strained.
- Do this exercise with caution if you recently had a knee injury or serious problems with your lower back, hips, and spine.
- Seniors with degenerative disk disease, back injury, and back pain should do this with caution.
- If you find it difficult to hold your inner thigh for any reason, use a yoga strap to reduce the strain. Also, put a blanket or two under your head if it's difficult to rest it comfortably on the floor or mat.

Cat-cow Pose

Get on your hands and knees with your wrist aligned with your shoulders, and knees aligned with your hips—your back should be in a neutral position.

On inhale, press your lower back downwards so that your tailbone sticks up. Keep engaging your abdominal muscles as your belly drops by drawing your navel into your spine. Lastly, gently lift your head to look at the ceiling without straining your neck.

On exhale, tuck your tailbone in by lifting your pelvis. Your back should be rounded as you draw your navel towards your spine. Bring your gaze down and look towards your navel to feel a stretch in your neck. Do this for about 5-10 breaths, and on your last exhale, return to a neutral position.

If you have knee discomfort, an alternative to this is to repeat the same movements on a chair with your hands placed gently on your knees.

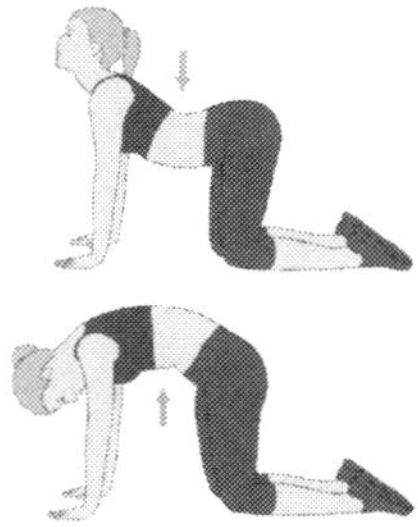

Easy Twist

Sit with your legs crossed in front of you, similar to the easy pose. Keep your back straight with your palms resting on your knees.

Place your right hand behind you, your left hand on your right knee, and twist to the right. Hold this position for 40-60 seconds and repeat on the other side. Do this for 3 reps.

If you have arthritis, back injury, or scoliosis, you may want to exercise a bit of caution when doing this stretch.

Downward Facing Dog

Start on your hands and knees with your palms slightly in front of your shoulders. As you inhale, lift your knees off the floor with your sit bones pointing towards the ceiling. Your palms should remain firmly placed on the floor.

On exhale, straighten your knees by pushing your heels towards the ground, and you should feel a stretch in your legs. Your heels don't have to fully touch the floor, but you should bring them as close as possible.

Warrior 1

Stand on your feet and put your left foot behind your right foot—there should be a considerable distance between your feet. Generally, your feet should be aligned on the mat, but for the sake of balance and comfort, you can place your legs wider (your form should be similar to a lunge).

Bend your right knee as close to 90 degrees as possible. Your left leg should be straight behind you as you turn your left heel to about 45 degrees.

As you inhale, bring your hands over your head, pressing your palms together, and slightly lift your head to gaze at your hands. Breathe in and out as you hold for 60 seconds. Switch to the other side.

Lunge Stretch

Get on your mat and start in a half kneeling position. Your right knee should be bent in front of you at a 90 degree angle, with your left knee slightly behind your hips. Both legs should be aligned.

Sink into your right knee—your foot should remain nice and flat on the ground. Take big deep breaths and go deeper into the stretch if you can. After 30 seconds, switch and repeat on the other side. Do this for 2 reps.

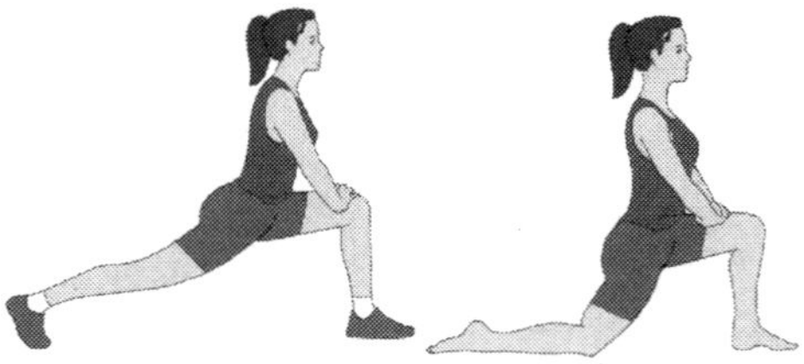

Cool-down Exercises

Child's Pose

Start on your hands and knees with your knees spread wide and legs tucked under your thighs.

Crawl your fingers forward until your arms are stretched in front, and rest your forehead on the mat or floor. If resting on your forehead isn't comfortable, turn your face to the side.

Take deep breaths and stay in this pose for as long as possible. For a variation, bring your arms beside you, close to your thighs, with palms facing upward.

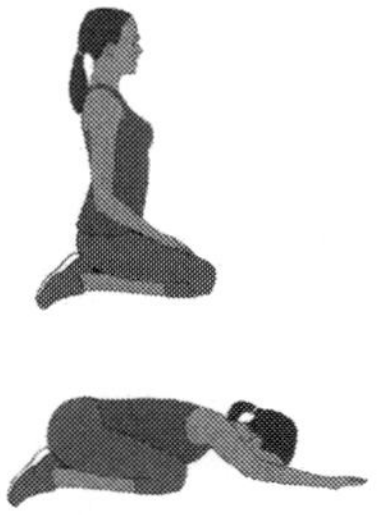

Cobra Stretch

Lie flat on your belly with your arms beside you. Your legs should be straight and slightly apart. Bring your palms forward and place them firmly on the floor beneath your shoulders. Use your arms to bring your chest off the floor—your arms should be completely straight.

Only your chest to the navel should be off the mat, and you don't have to straighten your arms fully if doing so strains your back. Hold for about 60 seconds while taking deep, steady breaths. Release this pose by slowly lying on your belly again.

Seated Single-leg Hamstring Stretch

Sit on the floor or mat with your legs extended in front of you. Tuck your left leg into the thigh of your right leg.

Lean forward until you're holding your foot or ankle, depending on your level of flexibility. If you can't reach either, stop when you feel a stretch. Hold the position for 30 seconds and switch to the other side. Do this for 3 reps.

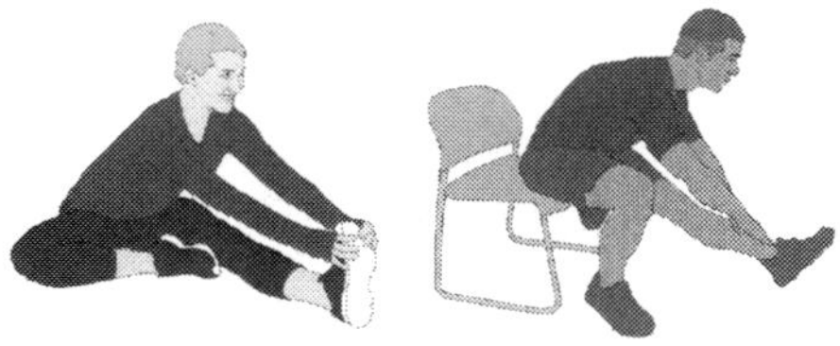

Standing Quad Stretch

Stand straight with your feet hip-width apart. Engage your abdominal muscles and keep your body relaxed. Bend your left knee, bring your heel towards your bum, and use your right hand to hold it. Stay in this position for 30 seconds, then switch sides.

If it's difficult, hold your left foot with your left hand or support yourself with a chair, then repeat the same stretch on your other foot.

Seated Forward Bend

Sit on your mat with your back straight and your legs in front of you. Gently use your hands to take hold of the balls of your feet. If this proves difficult, hold your ankles or the upper part of your feet. Lean forward and bend your elbows to get more of a stretch. You don't need to bend your elbows if that causes you pain.

Hold it for 30 seconds, release and repeat.

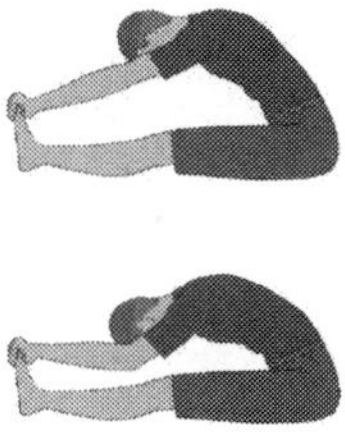

Knee-to-chest Pose

Lie on your back with your body perfectly straight, arms spread beside you. On exhale, bring both your knees to your chest and use your hands to hug your knees.

Rock slightly from side to side to release the tension in your back or stay still if it's difficult to move. Breathe slowly in this position and hold for 40-60 seconds.

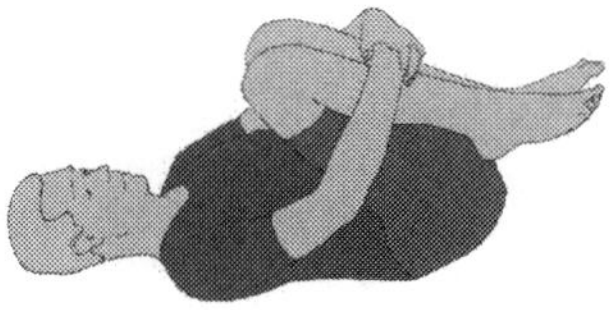

Shoulder Stretch

You can do this stretch either standing or sitting on a chair. Stand or sit with your legs shoulder width apart. Move your right arm across the front of your body, with your left arm firmly placed on your right elbow.

Hold for 20 seconds and switch to the other side. Do this for 3 reps on both arms.

Standing Forward Bend

Stand straight with your feet together. As you inhale, bend, and bring your hands down next to your feet or in front of you—use your hips to make the movements ensuring your back remains neutral. If you can't reach the ground, get into the pose, and stop when you feel a bit of tension without being uncomfortable.

Stay in this position for 30 seconds, standing straight without rounding your upper back or rolling your shoulders.

Corpse Pose

Lie flat on your back with your legs spread out and your arms beside you. Take deep breaths and wiggle different parts of your body to release any tension.

Stay in this position for 1-2 minutes.

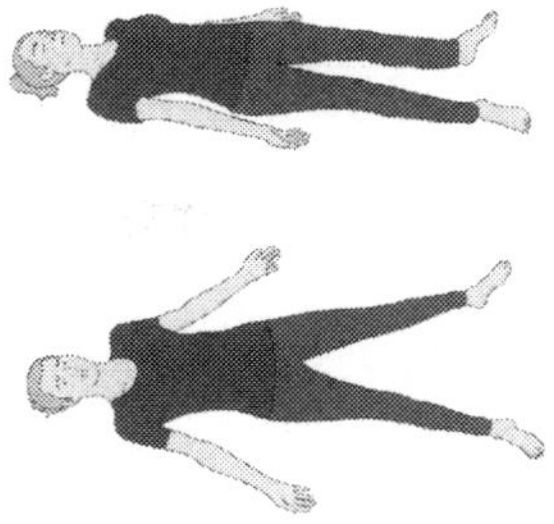

Mountain Pose

Stand tall with your legs hip width apart or bring your big toes together while your heels remain separate. Spread your toes, allowing them to stay firm but soft on the floor. Your arms should be slightly away from your body with palms facing forward.

Keep your abdominal and lower body muscles engaged to make sure you are standing upright, and ensure that your spine is in a neutral position.

Every part of your body should be perfectly aligned as you breathe and hold for a minute.

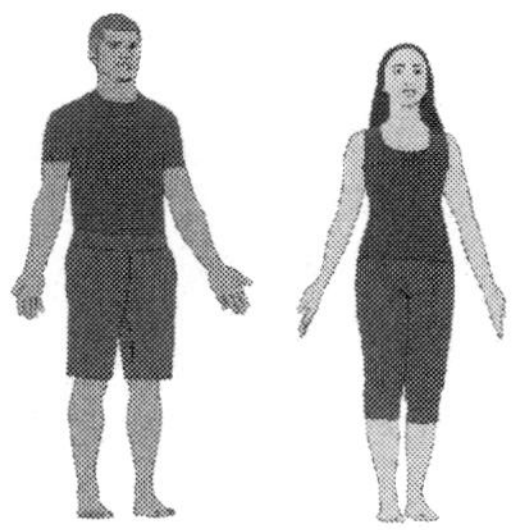

ONE WEEK STRETCHING ROUTINE

COOL DOWN STRETCHES					
1 & 5	Standing Quad Stretch	Standing Forward Bend	Shoulder Stretch	Cobra Stretch	Child's Pose
2 & 4	Knee To Chest Pose	Corpse Pose	Seated Forward Bend	Seated Single Leg Hamstring Stretch	Cobra Stretch
3 & 6	Child's Pose	Cobra Stretch	Standing Quad Stretch	Shoulder Stretch	Mountain Pose
7	REST DAY				

Key Takeaways

- Don't neglect stretching exercises. Like strength training and cardio, they are also very important.
- You will only feel the impact of stretching when it's done regularly.
- Stretching before a workout prepares your body to perform more demanding exercises, reducing the chance of injury.

Starting Strong

- Which of these exercises do you plan on adding to your stretching routine?
- Make a note of how you feel after one week of stretching.

CHAPTER 7:

EXERCISE SAFETY TIPS

- **Start with form:** if you are new to strength training, the best way to start out is to use lighter weights, focusing on keeping your body aligned and in the right position. Choosing more resistance than your body can handle will lead to straining during workouts, moving incorrectly, and increase the possibility of injuries. Focus on making controlled, smooth movements, and once you have it down, you can add more resistance to challenge your muscles.
- **Select the correct weight:** select a weight that allows you to complete the required number of repetitions and sets but remains challenging. It is always better to start with a lighter weight and increase the weights as you progress.
- **Choose different weights to challenge the right muscles:** have different sets of weights or resistance bands depending on the level of intensity needed to challenge your muscles. When finding it difficult to complete a set, you can switch to lighter weights or add some more weight if you're finding it easy to complete the workout.

- **Remember to breathe:** when feeling the strain from the exercise, it's easy to forget to breathe, but breathing is just as important as the exercises you are doing because it keeps your blood pressure from rising. Exhale when doing the exercise, and inhale when you are releasing the form.

- **Rest between sets:** this gives your muscles a chance to recuperate from their exertion and enables them to perform optimally during the next exercise.

- **Work hard and rest well:** practice upper body strength training about two to three times a week, giving your body at least 48 hours to heal and recover before going at it again.

- **Repetitions and sets:** the suggested repetitions and sets given below are appropriate for a beginner in reasonable health. However, if you find any suggestion either too easy or difficult, simply adjust it to suit your current physical capabilities. As your fitness improves, adjust each move accordingly to ensure the exercise is 'doable' but still remains challenging.

Note: The repetitions and sets in the exercises that follow are there to help; you can perform them individually, or as a routine when the time comes for you to create your program. It doesn't reflect in the eight-week program because it's timed, and done in a way to help you achieve up to 15 minutes of exercise every day.

With the safety tips covered, let's get into the exercises.

Upper Body Exercises

Training your upper body to be strong is crucial for your overall health because of its long-lasting effects. A little resistance gotten by adding weights to your fitness routine goes a long way in protecting your heart. By strengthening your cardiac muscles, the risk of heart attack and artery damage is lowered, and the oxygen levels in your blood are also increased. If you slouch or find it hard to walk straight, training your back helps to improve your posture by strengthening the muscles that support your body. Plus, having a strong upper body shields your body from musculoskeletal injuries or injuries that would have resulted from poor posture.

Furthermore, strengthening your upper body makes other activities easier. You have better coordination and balance no matter what you're doing, activities like swimming and running become easier, and your body burns more calories which helps you maintain a stable weight.

For the sake of clarity, the upper body refers to your chest, shoulders, forearms, and hands. Upper body exercises are designed to target the specific muscles in that area, such as your triceps, biceps, pectoralis (pectoral muscles), and shoulder muscles. Before you get into the habit of exercising your upper body, it is crucial that you understand how to do it safely.

Strength Training Exercises

Bicep Curls

Stand tall with your legs hip-width apart and dumbbells of your choosing in front of you. Pick the dumbbells up, and while holding them, your palms should be facing forward with your back straight.

On exhale, curl your elbows forward and bring the weights closer to your chest. When doing this, only your elbows should be moving—your upper arms and shoulders should remain relaxed.

Inhale and return to the starting position. Do 1-2 sets of 10 curls on each side.

You can do this exercise seated, depending on your preference.

Overhead Triceps Extension

You can do this exercise either sitting or standing, and your weights should be appropriate because dumbbells that are too heavy will make this exercise difficult and may lead to a loss of correct form.

Start by standing straight with a pair of dumbbells in your hands, and your feet hip width apart. Raise the dumbbells overhead and bend your elbows to lower the weights down. Hold for a moment, then bring the dumbbells back overhead by straightening your elbows.

5 Repetitions

2 Sets

As you progress and the exercise becomes easier, increase the number of reps to 10.

Remember to keep the movements slow and controlled, and engage your abdominal muscles to keep your body straight.

Palms-up Wrist Curl

Sit on a bench or chair and hold a dumbbell in your hands with your palms facing forward. Rest your forearms on your knees and use your wrists to extend the dumbbells downward. There should be little to no movement in your forearms, with your wrists performing most of the movement.

Use your wrists to raise the dumbbells up again and repeat.

10 Repetitions

2 Sets

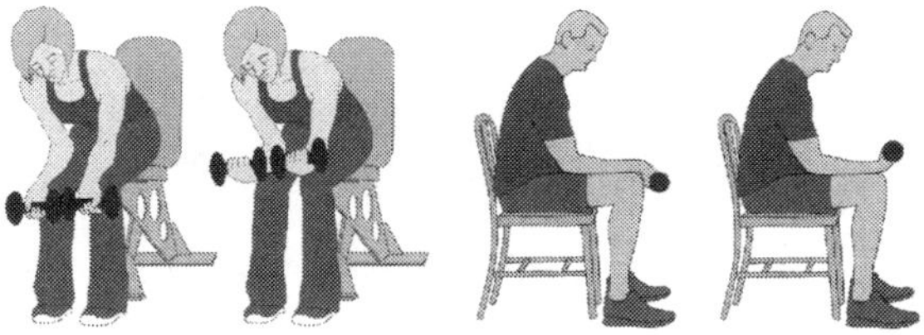

Alternating Dumbbell Punches

Start by standing with light dumbbells in each hand with your knees slightly bent for support; bring your fists close to your face as if you were guarding your it. As you throw your left punch, slightly rotate your abdomen to the right with your left leg somewhat straight.

Return your left arm to its neutral position, then repeat with your right arm.

10 reps on each arm

Chest Press

Start by lying flat with your feet on the floor. Your lower back shouldn't be arching—as if you are pulling your tummy button in.

As you exhale, raise your arms up with your palms facing forward. Your arms should be fully extended, and the dumbbells shouldn't be touching each other. Slowly bring them down to your chest as you inhale.

5 Repetitions

2 Sets

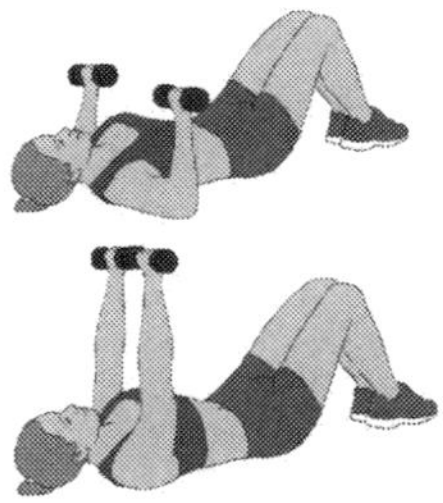

Lateral Raise

Start with your feet shoulder width apart with a slight bend in your knees. Pick your dumbbells up—your elbows should be slightly bent.

Slowly raise your arms simultaneously to the side until they form a T-shape with your body. Your arms should be parallel to the floor. Hold for a second, exhale, then drop your arms.

5 Repetitions

2 Sets

Slowly lower your weights to the floor after each set

When doing this exercise, your shoulder muscles are the center of attention. Use light weights as a beginner because you want to keep bouncing to a minimum. Also, keep your neck straight and look forward in order to avoid neck strain, and maintain a neutral spine.

Alternating Dumbbell Arm Raises

Stand straight with your feet hip width apart with dumbbells in both hands. On exhale, raise your right hand while keeping your left hand beside you—your hand should be parallel to the floor.

Hold this for a moment, then slowly drop your right hand. Repeat on the other side.

10 Repetitions

2 Sets

Use your arms and shoulders to do the movement and avoid swinging your body as much as possible (choosing comfortable weights help to achieve this).

Shoulder Press

Start with your feet hip width apart with dumbbells in both hands. Raise the dumbbells up to your shoulders with your palms facing forward.

Your elbows should be bent to form a 90 degree angle, and your upper arms should be parallel with the floor—this is the starting position.

In this position, exhale and push the dumbbells. Hold for a second, then slowly return your arms to the starting position as you inhale.

5 Repetitions

2 Sets

Cactus Arms

Stand on the mat with dumbbells in both hands and feet hip width apart. Bring your elbows together in front of you so that your elbows and arms form a 90 degree angle.

In this position, move your arms to the side while maintaining a 90 degree angle with your upper arms parallel to the floor. Hold for a moment, then bring your elbows back together.

10 Repetitions

2 Sets

Give your arms a break by dropping them down after the first set for 30 seconds before beginning the second set.

Toning Upper Body Exercises (without weights)

The exercises in this category require no weights, but you can hold small dumbbells if you want a bit of resistance.

Big Arm Circles

Stand with your feet shoulder width apart and bring your arms out to the side, parallel to the floor.

Make small motions by circling your arms, gradually making bigger circles.

Perform this exercise clockwise for 30 seconds, then anticlockwise for another 30 seconds. Drop your hands for a 10-20 second rest before repeating it.

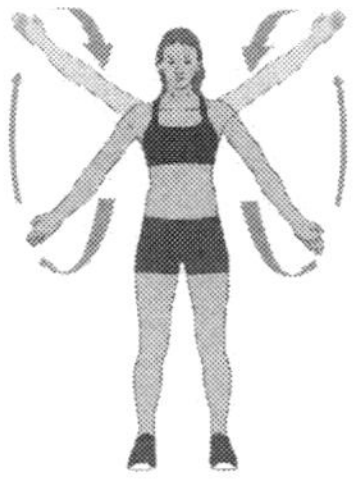

Plank Shoulder Taps

Get into a high plank position—your feet should be hip width apart with your wrists under your shoulders. To get into a high plank position, start by getting on all fours with your hands directly beneath your shoulders. Straighten your legs one at a time, lifting your knees off the floor; your hands should remain straight. Your back should be straight, and your bum shouldn't be poking out.

In this position, lift your right hand to touch your left shoulder, and return it to the ground. Then, use your left hand to touch your right shoulder.

Do this for 40 seconds.

Tricep Dips

For this exercise, place a chair or bench behind you. Sit on the chair, placing your hands by your sides, and step away from your chair. Your back should be barely touching the bench, and your arms should be straight. To make it a bit more difficult, you can step further away from the chair, but still keep your back close to it.

In a slow, controlled manner, use your arms to lift your body up and down—the entire movement should be done by your arms in order to work your triceps.

5 Repetitions

2 Sets

Forward Rotation

Stand straight with your chest out and feet hip width apart. Spread your arms straight beside you, parallel to the floor, and make big circles by rotating your arms.

Gradually bring your arms to the front without stopping the movement, then return them back to the side.

Repeat this motion for 60 seconds.

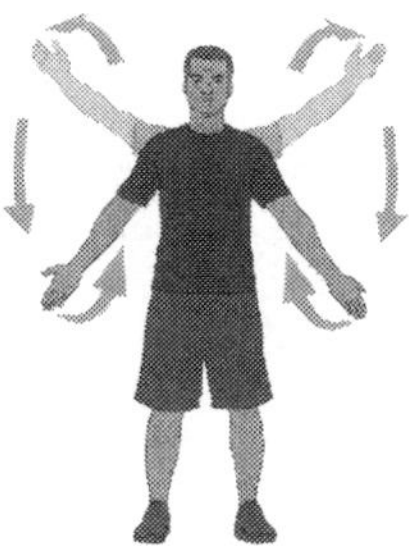

Plank Up and Down

Get into a high plank position—to get into a high plank, rest on all fours with your hands directly beneath your shoulders, then straighten your legs to lift your knees off the floor, keeping your wrists directly under your shoulders and your back straight. Your core and glutes should be engaged to provide stability, with your feet hip width apart.

Slowly lower your right arm so that your forearm is resting on the ground (like a low plank) and bring your left arm down as well. Straighten your arms and return to a high plank—that is one rep.

5-10 Repetitions

When doing this exercise, your body should remain still; you can spread your feet further apart if you need extra support.

Arm Pulses

You can either sit or stand for this exercise—when sitting, cross your legs in front of you and keep your back straight.

Stand or sit and bring your arms beside you—keep them straight and parallel to the floor.

1. Start by turning your palms to face the ceiling and move them upwards. Let your arms move slightly when doing this, about six to nine inches.

2. Next, turn your palms down to face the ground, and move them in that direction.
3. Then, turn your palms to the back facing the wall or space behind you, and slap them in that direction.
4. For the last step, face your palms forward and pulse in that direction.

Repetitions: Do each step for 20 seconds before moving to the next one—these four steps together make a set. Take a short rest between sets if needed.

2 Sets

Knee Push-up

This exercise is great for beginners new to pushups. Start in a high plank position with your hands slightly wider than your shoulders. Slowly drop your knees, keeping your back and hands straight—tighten your core and abdominal muscles to keep your body straight from your head to your knees. Another way to do this is to lie flat on your belly with your hands bent beside you, slightly wider than your shoulders. Use your arms to lift your upper body, and tighten your glutes and abdominal muscles to keep your body straight.

Keeping your gaze on the ground, slowly lower down by bending your elbows without rounding or arching your back. Pause when you're a few inches away from the floor, then straighten your arms again to return your body to its starting position. It is important that your hands do all the work while your body remains stiff. Exhale as you go down, and inhale as you bring yourself back up again.

5-10 Repetitions: Start with 5 reps if you are a beginner, and aim for 10 reps as you become comfortable with the exercise.

2 Sets

Arm Scissors

Stand with your feet shoulder width apart with your arms stretched out beside you; remember to keep your back straight.

Bring your arms in front of you, crossing your right arm over your left to form the letter X. Return your arms to the side and repeat, this time crossing your left arm over your right. Do this for 60 seconds.

Key Takeaways

Upper body exercises strengthen and tone your arms, shoulders, chest, and back.

- Give your body about 48 hours to rest and heal before going at it again.
- Take it slow and steady as a beginner, and don't be in a hurry to use heavier weights if you aren't ready for it.

Starting Strong

- Take note of the dumbbells or alternatives you have lying around the house that can be used, and determine your starting weight.
- Do you prefer upper body exercises without weights or those that require some weights? Start with exercises that match your preference but change the exercises regularly to keep your workout fresh, continuing to challenge your muscles.

CHAPTER 8:

CORE/BELLY FAT EXERCISES

A solid core gives your entire body stability, welcoming you into a life where your body is better balanced. These exercises are vital for preventing falls, reducing back discomfort, and restoring your body's youthful freedom.

The good news is that you don't need a gym membership to perform core exercises, as simple and safe core workouts can be performed at home. These workouts strengthen and tone your abdominal muscles, making your body feel better.

Why Is It So Crucial to Do Core Exercises?

Core strength is important for everyone, but it is especially important for seniors since it helps with posture, balance, and overall health. Your core consists of roughly 30 muscles, in addition to your abdominal muscles. This encompasses anything that has to do with your pelvis or spine.

I'm sure you're intrigued about the other muscles that make up your core, which include your upper and lower back muscles, oblique muscles, glutes (bum), and so on. These muscles are required for you to efficiently carry out basic daily activities from walking, jogging, playing tennis or golf, to cleaning the house.

A strong core:

- **Equals a balanced body**

Falling and losing your balance as a senior is unfortunately a common occurrence. Your physical condition may have deteriorated over the years to the point where you are continually unstable when walking, or you may now require the assistance of a walking stick. However, strengthening your core muscles will help you maintain balance, and this improved stability reduces the risk of falls and bolsters self-confidence.

Harvard Health has backed this information, claiming that by strengthening your core, your body will improve, allowing you to move it more effectively, with better control (Publishing, 2012). Your body will develop a sturdy trunk as a result of frequent core exercises, and your balance will improve dramatically.

- **Improves your posture**

The human body, like building structures, has a foundation and pillars, and your core functions as the central pillar that holds the entire body together. When your core is weak, your chances of slouching increase, and you may find yourself battling lousy posture, which is frequently difficult to modify.

As you become older, it's natural to lose some muscle mass. However, doing nothing to combat this loss is a bad strategy. As a result, doing core workouts improves your posture, protects your body from the effects of muscle loss, and enhances your overall health.

It is hard to overstate the benefits that core exercises deliver especially for seniors. They are simple and can be performed at home without expensive exercise equipment.

If possible, try to include core exercises in your workouts three or four times a week.

Belly Fat Loss in Seniors

Your body complains about body fat because it causes more harm than good to your essential organs, just as you worry about belly fat making you look out of shape, and it can cause health issues if left uncontrolled.

It's crucial to remember that as the human body matures, it's natural for body fat to migrate to your midriff. While this is an uncontrollable process, lifestyle choices have a huge impact on how much fat develops around your midriff. What is the best way to get rid of tummy fat?

Making good living choices is the first step toward losing abdominal fat. Some of these options are:

Eat Less When You're Stressed

Are you a person who eats when they're anxious or stressed and unsure why? Try to refrain from the huge bowl of ice cream and chocolate as the cure for a rough day at work. If possible, avoid comfort eating whenever possible, or at the very least reduce the portion size.

It's been scientifically shown that when you're anxious, your body desires high-fat, high-sugar foods (Peters, 2019). However, the problem is that these fats accumulate in the one spot we tend to despise the most: the midriff. This isn't a gender issue, as stress eating might equally cause a thin woman or a muscular man to gain weight.

When you are subjected to high levels of cortisol, you build belly fat, which cannot be eliminated solely by ignoring stress. Stopping stress-eating right now is easier said than done, but try to reduce stress whenever possible. If you want to eat to relieve stress, choose fruits and vegetables. If you eat well, you'll be able to achieve your aim of losing belly fat.

Muscle Development

Nobody is advising you to look like Dwayne Johnson when you're in your forties, fifties, or sixties, however it is crucial that you maintain muscle mass, and by extension lose belly fat, by exercising two to three times per week to maintain an active lifestyle.

This is confirmed by research published in the Journal of the American Medical Association in 2003 which noted that women who exercised for at least half an hour daily were measured with a six percent reduction in belly fat (Irwin et al., 2003a). And depending on how much exercise they got, that number rose further. In addition, engaging in muscle-building workouts when combined with a healthy diet leads to a reduction of harmful fat twice as fast as someone solely on a diet.

Many seniors believe that you cannot build muscle in your senior years, or that you have to go to the gym to regain muscular mass. Neither is true, as a thirty-minute walk, a mild jog, or regular home workout is sufficient.

Healthy Eating

Protein should be consumed in the amount of 70 grams per day because it strengthens your bones and muscles. Eggs, lean meat or fish, and skinless fowl are all good choices. Consume more fruits and fiber. Increase your intake of veggies and legumes. They keep your intestines in good shape, and because they take longer to digest, you are less likely to overeat.

In addition, healthy fats are an essential part of any diet for strong bones and a healthy heart. These healthy fats are high in antioxidants, which lowers your risk of contracting cancer. Omega-3 fatty acids are among these fats, and they should account for at least 20% of your diet.

Several foods should not be included in your diet: candy, cola, chips, cake, and cookies are good examples. If you have a strong need for deep-fried meals, try to indulge just once a month, including fast food. Reduce your intake of bread and other snacks as well.

Core Exercises

Here, we will be looking at examples of core exercises that can be done in the comfort of your home.

Seated Core Exercises

Knee-To-Chest (seated)

Sit down on an armless chair with your knees bent and your feet firmly on the floor.

Keep one foot flat on the floor while drawing the knee of your other leg to your chest, holding this position for 20-30 seconds.

Return to the beginning posture by relaxing and lowering the knee. Repeat with the opposite leg.

Repeat the exercise 5 times.

It is important to note that if the knee-to-chest exercise causes back or leg pain, stop immediately, and select another core exercise.

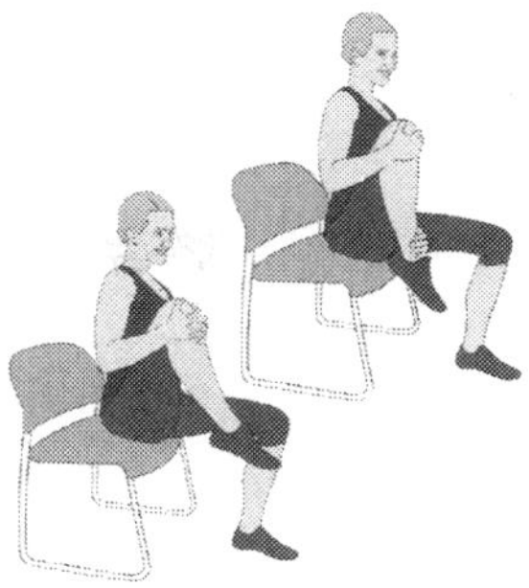

Leg Kicks

Begin by sitting on a chair or bench with your hands resting at the side of it. Your spine should be straight without any slouching.

Slowly raise your left knee so it's slightly higher than your right knee and straighten your leg. When straightening your leg, add some force to it as if you were kicking something away. Drop your left leg and repeat on the other side.

5 Repetitions

2 Sets

Add some ankle weights if you want to make it challenging.

Twists

During this exercise, ensure that your stomach and back muscles are constantly engaged.

Keep your legs crossed for added stability.

Avoid slouching or curving your spine by keeping it straight.

Allow your attention to follow your hands' movements.

- **Doing the twists**

Start by keeping your feet on the floor with your knees bent at a 90 degree angle.

Intertwine your fingers, or grip your hands together and straighten them out in front of you.

Turn to the right, then to the center, and finally to the left using your abdominals; that is one rep. To make it more intense, progress to Russian Twists, described below.

10 Repetitions

2 Sets

Leg Taps

Lie on a comfortable surface like a yoga mat, and keep your hands beside you with your palms facing the floor. Pull your legs inwards, bending your knees, with your feet firmly placed on the mat.

Use your core or lower body to lift your legs off the ground into a tabletop position. Return your legs to the ground with your feet slightly touching the floor before bringing them to the tabletop position again.

10 Repetitions

2 Sets

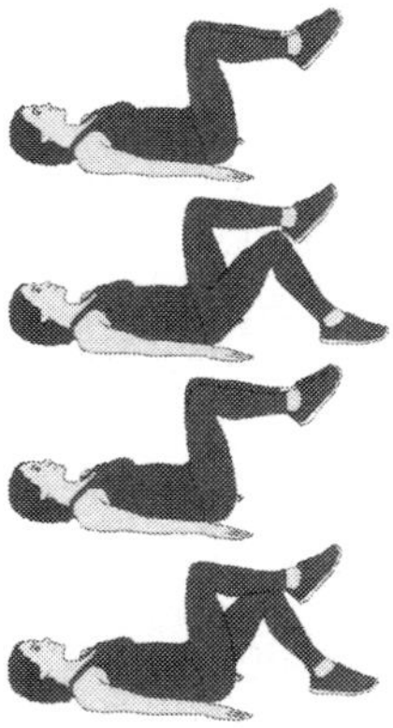

Side Bends

Sit on a chair.

Place one hand at the back of your head and slowly bend to the opposite side as if you're picking something up off the floor.

Reverse the process and do the same with the other hand, that is one repetition.

10 Repetitions

Mat Core Exercises

Forearm Plank

From a push-up position, bend your arms at the elbows so that your weight is supported by your forearms.

Tighten your glutes, compress your abs, and stretch your body out fully so that your back and legs are straight (in a lower plank).

Hold that position, starting with 20 seconds and progressively increasing the time as you become stronger.

Repeat as many times as needed: until you can no longer hold the position for the full amount of time without maintaining perfect form (your back should never dip down).

Modified Planks

Lie face down on the floor. Raise your body to the point where your forearms and knees are resting on the floor.

Then, ensure that your shoulders are directly above your elbows—your head and neck should align with your back.

Tighten your abdominal muscles.

Press your elbows and knees to the mat to create resistance. Neither of them should leave their position on the floor.

Take a deep breath, and hold for 30 seconds.

2 Repetitions

Glute Bridges

Lie on your back, with your knees bent and your feet firmly on the floor.

Maintain stability by putting your arms at your sides, your palms facing the ground for good balance.

Lift your hips until they make a straight line with your knees, hips, and shoulders, clenching your glutes hard and ensuring that your abs are drawn in.

Maintain this position for five seconds before returning to the starting position. This workout should be done at most three times a week.

5 Repetitions

2 Sets

Sit-ups

Lie on your back and place your feet flat on the mat, your hands touching your ears with arms bent at the elbow.

Lift your body up towards your knees as far as you can, then gently lower yourself back to the starting position. This exercise works your entire core, particularly your upper abdominal muscles.

5-10 Repetitions

2 Sets

Russian Twists

Begin by lifting your feet slightly off the ground while keeping your knees bent.

Extend and straighten your spine to form a V shape with your torso and thighs.

Before you begin, intertwine your fingers, or clasp your hands together and straighten them out.

Then, using your abdominals, slowly turn right, then center, and finally left.

5-10 Repetitions

2 Sets

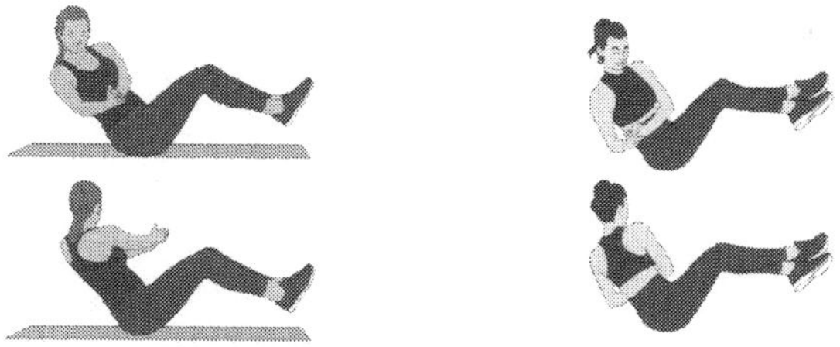

Reverse Crunch

Lie on your back with your arms at your sides, with palms down to help maintain balance.

To start, bend your knees and tighten your abs. Then lift your legs and bring your knees over your hips and towards your chest.

Tighten your abdominal muscles as you raise your legs.

You'll be using breathing exercises here: exhale as you raise your knees and hips to your chest. If your flexibility allows, ensure your hips leave the mat while you crunch your legs towards your chest, keeping your knees at a specific angle throughout the move.

Keep your knees at a specific angle throughout this exercise.

10 Repetitions

Superman

Lay face down on the mat with your arms stretched out in front of you.

Keep your core engaged and raise your lower and upper body from the floor, raising them as high as possible without hurting yourself.

Hold for two seconds, go back to step one, and be a Superman over again.

Note: this is a taxing exercise—**start with only a few reps** to avoid straining your body and build up the number of reps gradually over time.

5-10 Repetitions

Leg Lifts

Lay down with your lower back on the floor. Lift your legs until your back begins to leave the mat.

Keep your legs close together and engage your thighs.

Breathe in, then lower your legs gently back to the floor. Then, breathe out as you raise them again.

Note: if you allow your lower back to arch away from the mat, you are performing the exercise incorrectly and placing unnecessary strain on your back muscles.

Mountain Climbers

Assume a plank position ensuring that your weight is evenly distributed. Your hands should be placed directly beneath your shoulders with a flat back, your abdominal muscles engaged, and your head straightened.

Pull your knees one at a time towards your chest, alternating legs as if jogging in a plank position.

Ensure that your hips remain at a natural position, and continue in a smooth motion, alternating your legs as quickly as possible. Continue this exercise for 60 seconds

The exercises above build and strengthen your core, give your body better balance, and help to remove unhealthy

abdominal fats. However, it takes consistency to gain the desired result. Aim to perform these core exercises three to four times a week.

Being consistent is the key to any successful workout routine. Remember, Rome wasn't built in a day.

Key Takeaways

- Strengthening your core and abdominal muscles is key to maintaining your stability and freedom to go about your daily activities and do things that you love.
- Go slow and steady to see impressive results.
- Vary the core exercises you perform to challenge your core muscles in different ways.

Starting Strong

- Set aside fixed days and times to focus on building your core muscles.
- As your core gets stronger, increase the number of repetitions.
- Start with exercises you are eager to try out.

CHAPTER 9:

LOWER BODY EXERCISES

Your legs do a lot for your body. They help to perform daily activities like walking, running, dancing, and providing your body with enough balance and stability to prevent injuries and falls. Your lower body also provides support for some upper body movements; for instance, if you're reaching out to take something from the top of your wardrobe, you'll need to engage your lower body muscles as well. However, the lower body muscles are often neglected in favor of the upper body. While your upper body muscles do play a significant part in your wellbeing, the same can be said for your lower body. You are seeking a balance where your lower and upper body strength complement each other.

Lower body exercises target your glutes, hamstrings, quads, calves, and other muscles in the lower body region, allowing you to build strength, flexibility, and speed. When you perform exercises that allow you to focus on each leg, it enables you to correct any muscle imbalance, and give your nondominant leg much needed attention.

By exercising your lower body, hormones like cortisol that help to regulate metabolism and stress are released in large amounts. This helps you to relax and also pushes you closer to your fitness goals. For people with back pain as a result of tight hip flexors or weak hamstrings, exercising your lower body regularly can provide some relief, relieving these conditions in the long run.

Therefore, working out your leg muscles gives your body a strong foundation, and prevents your muscles from shrinking due to lack of physical activity, which many seniors suffer from. If your lower body continues to be neglected, it gradually becomes sore, loses muscle mass, accelerates the process of bone density loss, and increases your body's susceptibility to diseases and injuries. In a study done with men between the ages of 50 and 80, it was discovered that decreased muscle mass in the lower body led to impaired balance and increased the risk of falls.

From the above it is clear that exercising your upper and lower body is important, but of equal importance is that these exercises are done safely and with proper form. At the end of the day, the essence of working out is to help you feel your best after exercising and beyond. If you feel sore, consider skipping a day of leg exercises, or decrease the intensity of an exercise by reducing the number of repetitions performed. Alternatively, switch to low intensity exercises like yoga. If you want to work out with a mild issue like a sore throat or runny nose, be sure to reduce the intensity and number of repetitions of each exercise. However, if you have a more serious health issue, it is best to stop exercising for a period, rest, and give your body time to recover before resuming your workouts.

Give your muscles time to recuperate after every workout session. Pushing yourself too hard is likely to cause more harm than good. Don't forget to stretch afterwards, as it aids the healing process and allows your muscles to feel the full impact of the exercises.

Lower Body Exercises

Step Up

For this exercise, you'll need a sturdy strong box, a bench, a chair, or use of a staircase. When considering the height of the chair, bench, or box, it should be several inches below your knees or lower, depending on your comfort level. Also, ensure the surface of the chair, bench, or box is flat, stable, and strong enough to take your weight.

Place your right leg on the chair. The leg on the bench does all the work—with your weight on that leg, straighten it to lift your left leg up.

This exercise requires balance and stability. You can place your hands away from your body to provide some support, or place the chair, bench, or box close to a wall and use an outstretched arm to balance using the wall.

15 Repetitions each leg (complete the repetitions with your right leg before moving to your left leg).

Leg Extension

Sit on a chair or bench with your back straight. Your feet should be hip width apart with your hands placed beside you. Lift your left leg straight in front of you and hold it for 5-10 seconds. Drop the leg and repeat on the other side. For a challenge, get some light ankle weights to put more pressure on your legs.

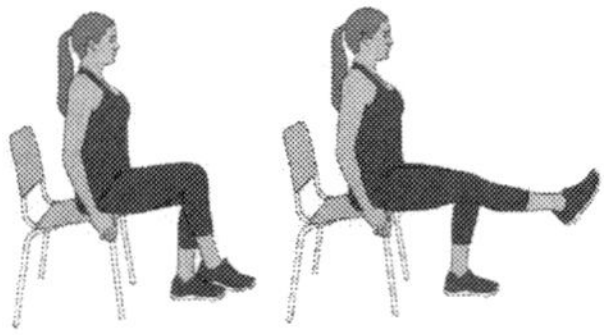

Leg Surrender

To do the surrender exercise, stand straight with your arms behind your head or in front of you in a prayer position. From there, bring your left knee to the floor or mat and bring your right knee down as well. Get back up by lifting your left knee off the ground followed by your right knee.

This exercise uses the strength in your legs to perform the movements, and it's advisable to take it slowly to avoid injuries. If it gets too difficult, use your arms to support your knees when getting up.

Heel Raises

Place a chair in front of you or stand in front of a wall for support. Stand behind the chair with your back straight, feet shoulder width apart, and hands lightly placed on the chair. Or stand in front of the wall with outstretched hands against it for support.

With your knees straight, lift your heels off the floor as much as you can without lifting your toes. Hold this position for five seconds, drop your heels, and repeat.

You can either lift both heels together, or alternate one at a time.

10 Repetitions

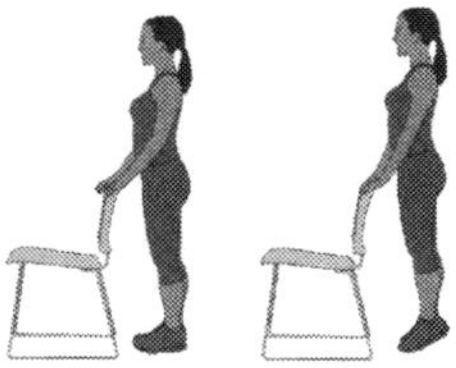

Chair Squat

Grab a chair or bench and place it behind you. Stand in front with your back straight and feet hip width apart—place your hands beside you. While standing, engage your core to provide some support, allowing the exercise to have more impact.

Bend your knees and lower your hips down until they come into contact with the chair. Then, without sitting on the chair, use your glutes to straighten your body back to a standing position. Your arms can be in a prayer position in front of your body, or you can straighten them out to provide balance.

Avoid rolling your back—your spine should remain neutral throughout this exercise.

10 Repetitions

Curtsy Lunge

This exercise requires balance, and you should focus on keeping proper form when doing this. Go slow but remain consistent.

To do this exercise, stand straight with your feet shoulder width apart with your arms resting beside you; don't forget to engage your core. Step your left leg behind you and place it in the opposite direction—your left and right legs should form a cross of sorts. Place your hands on your waist or in front of you, or in a prayer position for balance.

Slowly descend to the ground with your knees bent—your left knee should touch the floor. If it can't, get as close to the floor as you can without causing pain and hold it for a moment. Slowly straighten your legs to bring yourself back to the starting position, and repeat.

As you bend, your upper body should remain upright to feel the impact of this exercise.

5 Repetitions each leg (complete the repetitions with your right leg before switching to your left leg).

To increase the intensity of the exercise, you can either increase the number of repetitions performed, or hold hand weights.

Standing Side Leg Raise

Do this exercise while standing. For support, either hold on to the back of a chair in place, or move closer to a wall and use an outstretched hand against it.

Stand straight, place your hand on the chair or wall, and shift your weight to your left leg while lifting your right leg to the side. Bring your foot back down again and repeat.

As you straighten your legs, keep your back straight, and don't lock your knees. Although you may want to raise your leg as far as you can, overextending it could cause strain and injuries to your muscles. Try to raise your leg as far up as your range of motion allows before dropping it back down. Focus on doing the exercise with good form rather than increasing your speed.

10 Repetitions each (complete the reps on one leg before switching legs).

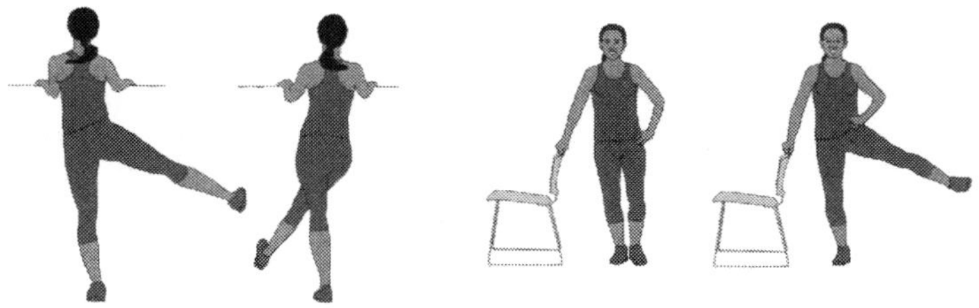

Reverse Lunge

Stand straight with feet shoulder width apart. Your hands can be at your sides, resting on your hips, or held in front of you in a prayer position. As you stand, take a large step back with your left leg. Your rear leg should be aligned with your right leg, and the toes of your left and right leg should be facing the same direction.

Slowly lower your body to the ground, with your right knee bent at a 90 degree angle, and your rear leg fully bent behind you.

Slightly touch the ground with your left knee before standing straight, or get as close to the ground as you can (without strain) before straightening your leg.

For some extra challenge, hold some dumbbells in your hands, or raise your hands over your head.

Note: only go as deep into the lunge as you can and try not to overdo it.

10 Repetitions each leg (complete the repetitions with your right leg before switching to your left).

Standing Hamstring Curls

Stand straight with feet hip width apart, hands placed on your hips or on a chair for support. Shift your weight to your left leg, slowly bend your right knee, and lift it from your heel to your bum. Hold this for a moment, then lower your leg.

To perform the seated alternative, get a resistance band and tie it to your couch or another object that won't easily move. Place your legs through the loop created and sit on a chair—there should be a bit of distance between the chair and the couch the resistance band is tied to.

In this position, straighten your legs out in front of you and bend your knees, pulling your heels to the back of your thighs.

10 Repetitions each leg (complete the reps on your right leg before switching).

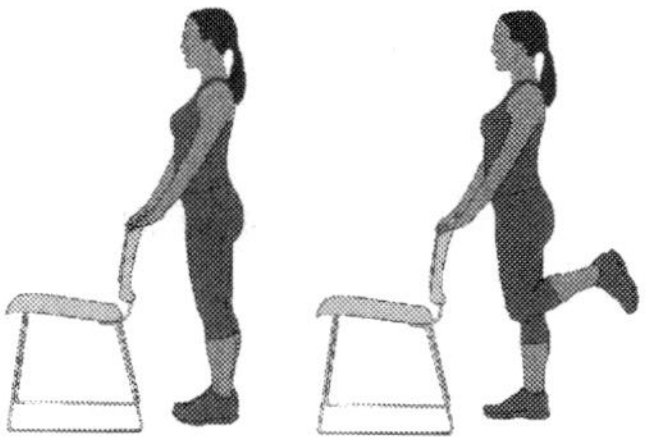

Toe to Heel

Place a chair in front of you or move close to a countertop for support. Standing at the back of the chair or in front of the counter, place your hands on it for support, and keep your spine straight with your gaze looking forward.

In this position, raise your heels off the floor as high as you can, and as you press your heels back to the ground, lift your toes off the floor.

10 Repetitions

2 Sets

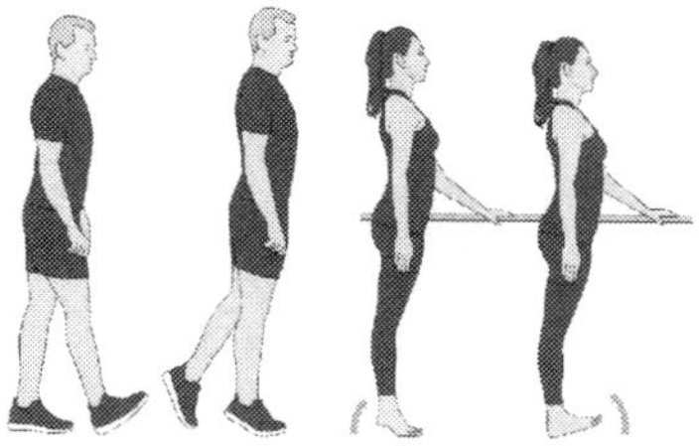

As you become comfortable with this exercise, you can switch things up by adding some walking. To do this, imagine that you are standing on a tightrope, and stretch your arms straight beside you for support—your legs should have some space between them.

When getting on the 'tightrope', place the heel of your left foot in front of you, holding the rest of your foot off the floor. Roll the foot to the ground and press the toes of your left foot down, lifting your heel off the floor as you bring your right foot in front of you, placing the heel on the ground. When placing your right foot to the front, there should be no space between your feet—both should be facing the same direction.

Lateral Lunge

Stand straight with your feet shoulder width apart. Take a big step to the side with your left leg, keeping your torso and back straight.

Then, slowly bend your right leg to a 90 degree angle while keeping your left leg straight; you can stay in this position for a few seconds or return back to the starting position. Switch to the other side.

5 Repetitions for each leg (complete the repetitions for your right leg before moving to your left).

March in place

Stand straight with your feet hip width apart, arms resting at your side. Bring your left knee as high as you can, drop it down, and switch to the other side. You can add some arm movements to it, or hold some dumbbells if you want to work your arms as well.

Imagine yourself in a marching band.

Get close to a wall if you want some support, and do this exercise ***30 times***.

Lateral Band Walk

For this exercise, you'll need a resistance band. You can either place the band above your ankles or above your knees, depending on your preference.

Stand straight and keep your feet a little wider than hip width. Slowly bend your knees until you come to a half-squat position. Your feet should remain in line with your shoulders, with your spine in a neutral position, facing forward.

In this pose, take a big step sideways with your left leg and bring it back to the starting position. Or, instead of bringing your left leg in, take your right leg closer to your left leg while keeping the distance between your legs.

15 repetitions each way, left and right.

Key Takeaways

- Lower body exercises are just as important as upper body workouts. A combination of both gives you a balanced, strong, and fit body.
- Beginners should go slow and pay attention to any existing health conditions before doing any of these exercises.

Starting Strong

- Do you already have a lower body routine in place? What modifications can you make to it based on the exercises in this chapter?
- For exercises like heel raises that initially require you to use support, try doing the exercises without reinforcement as your balance improves.

CHAPTER 10:

CARDIO EXERCISES

When most people hear the word 'exercise,' what immediately comes to mind is running, jumping jacks, high knees, burpees, and other exercises that get your heart rate up quite quickly—these are called cardio exercises. Cardiovascular or aerobic exercise is any physical activity that gets your heart rate up and keeps it up for a prolonged period of time. There are good reasons why cardio exercises are favored by many, and these benefits are particularly important as we age.

These benefits include:

- **Strengthening your lungs and heart:** increasing your heart rate increases the flow of blood and oxygen throughout your body and, in turn, tones your lungs and heart.
- **Helps to manage chronic conditions:** doing cardio workouts consistently supports your immune system and helps people with arthritis, high blood pressure, diabetes, and stroke. It also reduces the risk of some cancers, such as those of the breast, bladder, kidney, colon, and stomach. According to a study published in 2019, cardio workouts combined with other exercises reduced the risk of cardiovascular disease by 80%,

and there was also a 90% reduction in the risk of type 2 diabetes, and a 33% reduction in the risk of cancer (Thomas et al., 2021).

- **Promotes better sleep:** apart from improving your energy levels throughout the day, you'll find that doing cardio leads to a very satisfying night's rest, leaving you feeling refreshed and happy when you wake up in the morning. According to a study done in 2013, engaging in 30 minutes of cardio exercise improved the quality of sleep in people with insomnia (Baron et al., 2013). As we age we tend to sleep less, so for seniors, quality of sleep assumes an increasing importance for wellbeing.

- **Keeps off excess weight:** you gain weight when you consume more calories than your body burns—cardio resolves this by increasing your body's ability to burn calories, not only during the exercise itself but also after the workout. By doing at least 150 minutes of cardio per week, as recommended by the Center for Disease Control, you can maintain your current weight. To shed some excess pounds, you can always increase the amount of cardio, depending on your current weight and health needs.

- **Strengthens your bones and muscles:** doing cardio and strength training exercises in general lubricates your joints, and maintains and builds muscle mass, the latter being particularly important for seniors. Your hips and bones will thank you because cardio reduces the possibility of hip fractures and fall related injuries.

Living a long life comes with its perks but for you to continue to live a happy, satisfied, and independent life, combining cardio exercises with the different types of workouts and stretching discussed in this book helps to achieve that.

You'll be able to perform physical activities with ease, and experience greater mobility than inactive people.

As always, safety comes first, and your goal should be to balance the duration, frequency, and intensity of these exercises. Doing cardio for the first time can be a bit uncomfortable, but you can get into it by doing something you love before moving to more intense exercises. For instance, you can do light jogging, dancing, or other cardio exercises that you love. From there, you can progress to more challenging exercises.

Most cardio workout sessions give little rest time in between exercises to keep your heart rate up throughout the process, **so it's essential that you start at the right pace, speed, and intensity that's comfortable for you;** the goal is to keep growing from there.

If you find the suggested duration of an exercise too challenging simply reduce the duration and build week on week toward the suggested duration and period periods.

Every week, try to increase the amount of time you spend doing these exercises by about 5-10 minutes to push your body further. Also, to avoid plateaus and boredom, switch up your workout routine every four to six weeks, gradually increasing the intensity and speed. Take time to rest between workouts to allow your body to recover and rebuild.

Last but certainly not the least, talk to your doctor or healthcare professional before starting a new workout program.

The Exercises

Lateral Toe Taps

With your feet hip width apart, bend your knees slightly and get into a half squat position—remember to keep your spine neutral, and place your hands on your hips or in a prayer position in front of you.

Take a big step to the side with your right leg, and tap the floor lightly with your toes before bringing it back. Do the same on the other side.

Do this for 30 seconds with a 20 second rest, and repeat 3 times.

Skaters

Stand straight with your feet hip width apart, arms at your sides. Hop to the right, placing your left leg behind your right, and bringing your left hand in front of you. Hop to the left, positioning your right foot behind you, with your right arm to the front. If hopping makes it too challenging, do the exercise without the hop.

Do this for 30 seconds with a 20 second rest, and repeat 3 times.

Butt Kicks

Stand straight with your feet hip width apart and arms by your side. Bring your left heel close to your bum, drop it, and repeat on the other side.

What makes this exercise different from standing hamstring curls is the level of intensity and speed involved, as you'll be doing this without the support of a chair or wall. You can start slow, but as the exercise progresses, increase your speed and add a bit more force when bringing your heels close to your bum.

Do this for 30 seconds with a 20 second rest, and repeat 3 times.

Standing Scissors Jump

Stand with your right leg in front of you, arms at your sides or on your hips. Make a small jump and shuffle your left leg to the front while taking your right leg to the back; you can move your arms along with your body to increase the intensity of the exercise.

Do this for 30 seconds with a 20 second rest, and repeat 3 times.

Lateral Hops

If you have a yoga mat in front of you, stand at the end of one side. If you're doing this on the ground, make a small demarcation with paper tape between the left and right sides, because the goal of this exercise is to move from side to side.

Standing on the left side with your feet together and arms beside you, hop to the right side, then immediately hop to the left again, and repeat.

The goal of this exercise is to get your feet across the paper tape to the other side—you can lift your arms up for support. Go as fast as you can.

Do this for 30 seconds with a 20 second rest, and repeat 2 times.

Lunge Step-backs

For this exercise, stand with a slight bend in your knees with your feet hip width apart. Take a big step back with your left leg, then alternate with your right leg. Remain light on your feet by keeping your heels off the ground as you step back.

Also, you don't have to bend your knees to the floor like a normal lunge (imagine that you're running backward). You can hold some dumbbells for more resistance if needed.

Do this for 30 seconds with a 20 second rest, and repeat 3 times.

High Knees

Stand straight with your feet hip-width apart. Stretch your arms in front of you to serve as the target your knees should reach.

Bring your left knee up or try to let it touch your outstretched hand, drop it to the floor, then raise your right knee.

This exercise takes your heart rate straight up, and you should start slow if this is your first time doing it to avoid any strain. Gradually increase the pace as you get comfortable with high knees exercise.

If you wish to increase the exercise intensity, you can add a twist to it by moving laterally while doing the high knees. This will increase the level of difficulty, and you'll get a good sweat on.

Do this exercise for 30 seconds, rest for 20, and repeat.

Jump Rope (with or without rope)

Stand straight with your feet shoulder width apart, arms spread from your body as if you were holding a jump rope. Rotate your wrists and keep your feet together as you jump. To increase the intensity, jump front and back for a few seconds before returning to jumping on the spot.

If you want to use a jump rope, these can be purchased cheaply.

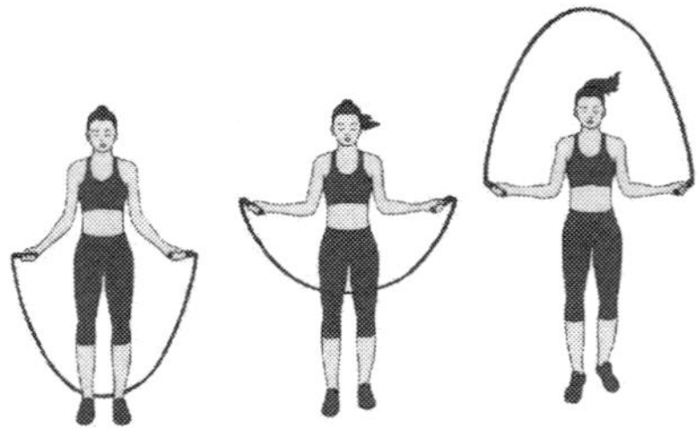

Pop Squat

Go down into a squat with your feet a little wider than shoulder width. To do the pop, jump up with only your heels leaving the floor. As you do this, bring your feet together.

To return to the squat, drop your heels to the floor and spread your legs wide as you return to the squat position—focus on keeping your back straight.

For an easier alternative, get into a squat position, hold it for a moment, then stand straight.

Do this exercise for 30 seconds, rest for 20, and repeat.

Star Squat

Get into a squat position with your spine in a neutral position. To get into the star pose, jump with your legs maintaining the same distance, with your arms straight above your head (resembling a star). Return to the original squat position, hold it for a second, and perform the star pose again. For an easier alternative, do the squats with some front kicks (put some power into the kicks to add to the intensity of the exercise).

Do this exercise for 30 seconds, resting for 20.

V Step

Stand with your feet slightly wider than shoulder width apart—your legs should be straight, forming a V shape.

Maintaining the distance between your legs, take a big step forward with your left leg and bring your right leg forward as well (as if you were taking big steps forward). Step back to the starting position and repeat. For more of a challenge, get into a half squat position as you make the movements. The key element to this exercise is speed, and you should do the steps as fast as you can.

Do this exercise for 30 seconds, rest for 20, and repeat.

Jumping Jacks

Stand with your legs straight and arms at your sides. Jump, spreading your feet wider than hip width apart, and bring your arms over your head. Jump back to the starting position, and repeat. For an easier alternative, rather than jumping, step to the side while raising your hands over your head as you move.

Do this exercise for 30 seconds, rest for 20, and repeat.

These are some great cardio exercises you can do as a warmup or a full body routine, but don't restrict yourself to them only. Go for a walk or run in the morning while listening to your favorite songs, or tend to your garden. In the evenings, go for brisk walks, or to a dance or aerobics class. To make it fun, do these exercises with a friend that will motivate you and continue to keep you accountable. I highly recommend that you have a fitness tracker when doing cardio exercises, as it is a great way to keep track of your progress and level of physical activity, both of which help with motivation.

To get the best out of these exercises, do them at least three days a week, using the remaining days to rest and recover. Above all remain consistent, and try to set new goals for yourself every month in order to see amazing results.

Key Takeaways

- Cardio exercises require balance, intensity, duration, and frequency based on your comfort level and current abilities. Go at your own pace, and as the exercises progress, increase the speed and intensity to get your heart rate up.
- The alternatives to the exercises are there to give you a strong foundation before doing something more intense. Start with those until you can maintain correct form, and your fitness and comfort level improve. When you feel ready, increase the intensity.
- Jogging, walking, gardening, and dancing are all valid forms of cardio exercise. Try to do them once in a while to switch up your cardio routine and prevent boredom.

Starting Strong

- On your first day, aim for 5-10 minutes of cardio, and regularly switch the intensity of the exercises as needed. Gradually increase the duration and intensity of your cardio workouts as your fitness improves.
- If you're using a fitness tracker, note the amount of calories burned, steps taken, and level of physical activity achieved. Try to surpass those numbers the following week by increasing the time spent exercising, or the intensity of the workouts.

CHAPTER 11:

EIGHT WEEK WORKOUT PROGRAM

The knowledge you've gained in the previous chapters was all leading to this moment—your very own eight-week workout program. This program is focused on helping beginners. and those who have little experience exercising, to get started and give you a solid foundation in order to do more advanced workouts. Before we get into it, let's do a short recap of what you need to do before starting the program:

1. **Choose a place and time:** having a certain place and time for your workouts eliminates half the struggle of getting started. So, before you get into any of the sessions, choose a corner of your house that has enough space for you to move comfortably.

2. **Do each six-seven minute workout twice per day. Personally, I prefer to run through each workout twice in one season instead of splitting it, but you can always repeat the same workout at a different time if that is more convenient for you. For instance, if you're working out in the morning, you can do the**

same routine in the evening, or a few hours before going to bed.

3. **Drink some water:** water is one of the few things you cannot do without when preparing for a workout. According to the American Council of Exercise, you should drink about 17 to 20 ounces of water two to three hours before starting your workout, and drink about 7 to 10 ounces of water within 10 to 20 minutes of exercise (Bernstein & Munoz, 2012). Drinking water during exercise prevents dehydration which can cause heat exhaustion, heatstroke, and tired muscles. Drink more water within 30 minutes of completing your session to keep yourself feeling refreshed after your workout. Depending on your consumption of water, you may want to have some refillable bottles of water beside you to have easy access when you need it. Drinking plain water can get a bit boring—you can add some flavor to it by adding some lemon or lime juice; adding these can also help to increase your metabolism.

4. **Determine your fitness level:** from the start, get an idea of how far you can go with the exercise to avoid overworking yourself. If you're running or walking, determine how far you can go before turning home. When performing stretching exercises, establish how deep into the stretch you can go without discomfort. For the exercises that come with alternatives, check if those substitute movements will be the best fit for you as a beginner. The goal is to acknowledge your starting level and strive to improve from there.

5. **Start slowly:** this cannot be emphasized enough. After determining your fitness level, start with the right intensity, then gradually speed up the pace of each exercise as your level of fitness improves. If you're find-

ing it a bit difficult to do any exercise at once, stop and take some time for a quick breather. Taking a break from a workout becomes more necessary if you're feeling dizzy, nauseous, experiencing shortness of breath, or pain in any part of your body. Talking about pain takes us to our next point.

6. **Have a timer:** for this eight-week program, it is advisable to set a timer on your phone for each exercise. Every drill takes about one minute, including rest time, and is done in seconds. Having a timer set helps to keep track of the time.

7. **Know the difference between good and bad pain:** it's tempting to want to give up on a workout session when it gets intense, but there is no gain without a bit of pain—at least to some extent. When working out, expect to feel some discomfort because it is a sign that you are putting the work in. For strength training exercises, your muscles will experience micro tears and burning sensations; these sensations indicate that your muscles are being challenged. As they heal, your muscles will build more strength to ensure that the tears don't happen again.

   For cardio exercises, pain can manifest in the form of 'jelly legs': a burning sensation in your lungs, tired muscles, and an increase in body temperature which will cause you to sweat profusely. Plus, you may find yourself gasping for air during and after the workout before your breathing returns to normal. This shows that enough stress is being placed on your body, causing it to recover and adapt. As we discussed earlier, your metabolism also gets a boost, and keeps you in fat-burning mode throughout the day.

   Now, what does bad pain feel like? This type of pain feels sharp, acute, and may exhibit itself in a specific part of your body. It doesn't reduce after the workout and may affect the way you go about your day. This type of pain indicates that your muscles were pushed far beyond their current capabilities, and continuing the workout, or doing it with the same intensity the day after, can lead to serious injuries and set you back a couple of days or weeks, depending on how serious the injury is.

Take some time to rest after every workout, but if you feel bad pain, you should give your body more time to recover so that it doesn't result in complications.

8. **Strive to make it a habit:** there is a famous quote by Jim Rohn, and it goes like this: "motivation is what gets you started, habit is what keeps you going"

   (*A Quote by Jim Rohn*, n.d.). Your health and fitness goals may be the driving force that push you to exercise now, but what happens when you hit your ideal weight and get the health benefits you were aiming for? What keeps you going then? How about on days when your sources of motivation are not even enough to get you out of bed? The only way you can continue moving forward and maintain those benefits is to make exercising a habit.

To make exercising a habit that will stick with you, let's look at the four laws of building habits set out by James Clear in his book Atomic Habits:

- **Make it obvious:** place your exercise routine as the next thing you do after a current habit. For instance, if you pray or meditate every day after waking up, make your workout session the next thing you do before continuing your day.

- **Make it attractive:** exercising should be something you want to do every day. To make it attractive, play some of your favorite songs, do the exercises with a friend(s), or take it as a time for some self-care.
- **Make it easy:** start with easy exercises that you can do with just the right amount of effort and try to do them as many times as possible. Create an environment where exercising is one of the easiest things to do, and reduce the distractions that can stop you from going through with your workout routine.
- **Make it satisfying:** having a satisfying experience when exercising makes it something you'll want to keep doing. To do this, you can start by doing exercises you enjoy to bring some fun into it. Seeing evidence of your progress is another way to make exercising satisfying, and it can motivate you to keep going.

By following these rules, your brain will gradually adapt to it and make exercising something you do automatically. With that covered, let's get into the program.

Weeks 1 & 2

WEEK 1 & 2							
Cardio Workout	Jumping Jacks (Alt)	Lateral Toe Taps	High Knees	Lunge Step Back	Lateral Hops	Butt Kicks	Jog In Place
Strength Training	Bicep Curls	Palm Up Wrist Curl	Chest Press	Reverse Lunge	Step Up	Chair Squat	Lateral Lunge
Lower Body Workouts	Step Up	Lunge	Reverse Lunge	Lateral Lunge	Squats	Toe To Heel	
Upper Body Workouts	Bicep Curls	Alternating Dumbbells Punches	Overhead Triceps Extensions	Shoulder Press	Lateral Raise	Arm Circles	
Cardio Workout	Jog In Place	High Knees (Alt)	Jump Rope	Pop Squat (Alt)	Star Squat (Alt)	Jumping Jacks	
REST DAYS							

Exercises	Time On (Seconds)	Rest (Second)
Cardio	40	20
Strength T	35	25
Lower Body	45	15
Upper Body	45	15

Instructions

- Include warmup and cool down exercises.
- Each exercise session takes about six to seven minutes and should be repeated twice daily in order to have the recommended effect.
- Increase the rest time if needed.
- Ensure you perform the exercises with proper form and technique.

- Strength training workouts require you to use dumbbells or their alternatives, but for the first two weeks, start with no weights or very light ones. They should include a combination of both upper and lower body exercises.

N.B: 'Alt' stands for alternative. This means you have the choice to do the alternative of each exercise mentioned.

Weeks 3 & 4

WEEK 3 & 4							
Cardio Workout	Jumping Jacks	High Knees	Skaters	Standing Scissors Jump	Butt Kicks	Jumping Jacks (Alt)	Lateral Toe Taps
Strength Training	Squats	Pop Squat	Shoulder Press	Lateral Arm Raise	Alternating Dumbbells Arm Raise	Heel Raise	Bicep Curls
REST DAY							
Lower Body Workouts	Leg Extension	Step Up	Curtsey Lunge	Standing Side Leg Raise	Standing Hamstring Curl	Standing Hamstring Curl (Alt)	
Upper Body Workouts	Plank Shoulder Taps	Triceps Dips	Arm Circles	Shoulder Press	Alternating Dumbbells Punches	Biceps Curls	Plank Up And Down
Cardio Workout	Lateral Top Taps	Lateral Hop	Butt Kicks	Pop Squats	Jumping Jacks (Alt)	High Knees	
REST DAY							

Exercises	Time On (Seconds)	Rest (Second)
Cardio	45	15
Strength T	40	20
Lower Body	45	15
Upper Body	45	15

Instructions

- For strength training, slightly increase the weight of the dumbbells you're using as your fitness level improves.
- Each exercise session takes about six to seven minutes and should be repeated twice daily in order to have the recommended effect.

- Focus on maintaining your form while increasing the intensity of the exercises.
- Include warmup and cool down stretches.
- Remember to track your progress.
- Take some measurements to compare at the end of the program.

Weeks 5 & 6

WEEK 5 & 6							
Cardio Workout	GO FOR A 15-20 MINUTES RUN OR WALK						
Strength Training	Overhead Arm Extension	Shoulder Press	Curtesy Lunge	Alternating Dumbbells Arm Raise	Lateral Arm Raise	Modified Plank	Plank
Lower Body Workouts	Leg Taps	Glutes Bridge	Step Up	Reverse Lunge	Leg Surrender	Bicycle Crunches	Sit Ups
REST DAY							
Upper Body Workouts	Plank Shoulder Tap	Triceps Dips	Arm Circles	Arm Scissors	Knee Push-Ups	Alternative Arms	Arm Pulses
Cardio Workout	Skaters	Leg Kicks	Jump Rope	Standing Scissors Jump	Lateral Hop	Jumping Jacks	
REST DAY							

Exercises	Time On (Seconds)	Rest (Second)
Cardio	45	15
Strength T	40	20
Lower Body	45	15
Upper Body	45	15

Instructions

- For the first cardio workout session you can use a treadmill, depending on your preference. If there's bad weather, you can switch it with the last day of cardio.
- Each exercise session takes about six to seven minutes and should be repeated twice daily to have the recommended effect.

- Have a fitness tracker or app on your phone to track steps and calories burned.
- Include day four of both warmup and cool down exercises.

Weeks 7 & 8

WEEK 7 & 8							
Cardio Workout	Pop Squat	Lunge Step Backs	Skaters	Jump Rope (Skips Back And Front)	Standing Scissors Jump	High Knees (With Lateral Movement)	Jumping Jacks (Alt)
Strength Training	Leg Surrender	Standing Hamstring Curls (Seated Alt)	Plank Up And Down	Lunge	Reverse Lunge	Bicep Curls	Plank
Lower Body Workouts	Knee To Chest	Leg Extensions	Bicycle Crunches	Heel Raises	Reverse Crunch	Lateral Lunge	Crunches
Upper Body Workouts	Knee Push Up	Overhead Arm Extensions	Alternating Dumbbells Punches	Arm Pulses	Triceps Dips	Palm Up Wrist Curl	Shoulder Press
Cardio Workout	**GO FOR A 15-20 MINUTES WALK/JOG**						
REST DAYS							

Exercises	Time On (Seconds)	Rest (Second)
Cardio	50	10
Strength T	45	15
Lower Body	50	10
Upper Body	50	10

Instructions

- If you have different sets of weights, start with medium size and go with your heaviest weights once your form is perfected.
- Each exercise session takes about six to seven minutes and should be repeated twice daily to have the recommended effect.

- For weeks seven and eight, reduce the number of times you do the alternative exercises.
- Include warmup and cool down stretching exercises.
- Take your measurements.

Key Takeaways

- Drink some water before, during, and after workouts to prevent dehydration, fatigued muscles, and cramping.
- For the first two weeks, focus more on correct form rather than increasing the intensity. If this is your first time using weights, start with the light ones and move on from there.
- The only way you can keep enjoying the benefits of exercise after this program has ended is to make it a habit. To do this, you need to make it obvious, easy, satisfying, and attractive.
- Having a timer set on your phone to keep track of the time is helpful.

Starting Strong

- Make a note of how you felt at the beginning of the program, and after the first two weeks. Compare this with your current fitness level and state of mind at the end of the program. Are there any significant differences?
- What healthy eating habits did you employ to reach your goals during the eight-week program?

CHAPTER 12:

DO-IT-YOURSELF WEEK

Having a program designed by someone else can be fun and challenging, but there is a certain level of satisfaction that comes from creating a plan of your own and sticking to it. When you want to get into shape or continue on your fitness journey, trying out your own fitness plan can be a step in the right direction.

It allows you to explore your interests and set new goals and challenges for yourself. For instance, if you want to lose 8kg in a month, you can use the knowledge gained from other workout programs to create something perfectly tailored to your needs. Plus, you can create a workout plan to fit your lifestyle and accommodate your schedule so that you can easily continue on your fitness journey. One major benefit to creating your own plan is that it can act as a source of motivation and fuel your drive to get fit. When you start something by yourself, there is an urge to see it through, and you'll feel proud of yourself when you succeed in it.

After all, no one knows you more than yourself, and a personalized workout plan is an expression of your personality. Whatever you find enjoyable, luckily, you get to do that in this chapter.

In this chapter, you'll be exploring some of your favorite exercises and bringing them together to form a workout plan. Since this exercise plan will be based on your personal preferences, it is meant to be fun and enjoyable, while getting you to your fitness goals. Before we go into it, let's lay down some ground rules:

- **Choose exercises you enjoy but make them challenging:** the purpose of this DIY section is for you to choose exercises you enjoy, but also challenge you. The only way to move forward is to set a limit or goal that you wish to pass, and by the time you exceed it, you'll automatically know that you've entered a new stage in your fitness level. Instead of choosing only easy exercises you like, try to add some challenging ones to mix things up a little.

  However, when considering challenging exercises, remember that your safety and health come first.

Also, this is where the repetitions and sets of each exercise becomes increasingly important. Remember to include the number of repetitions and sets for each exercise in the plan you create.

- **Have a variety:** Include a mix of cardio, strength training, stretching, and other forms of exercise in your routine. There will always be a tendency to prefer one type of exercise over another, but to reap all the health benefits of exercise, you have to give each one of them a chance to shine.

- **Include recovery days:** There were adequate recovery days in the eight-week program, but when you're creating something for yourself, you may want to push your body to the limit and overwork yourself; this rarely ends well. For this program, listen to your body and decide how much time you need to recover before you can go again.

- **Seek the help of a doctor if needed:** If you have any current health conditions that can benefit from certain exercises, or an issue that may affect the way you do certain exercises, it is advisable that you consider joining hands with your healthcare provider and consider those issues when designing your fitness plan.
- **Include outdoor activities for a change of scene:** Exercising in one place can become monotonous, and your body may appreciate a change of location. When creating your plan, don't restrict yourself to the exercises discussed in this book, as you can include others that allow you to enjoy the outdoors like walking, jogging, gardening, and many more.
- **Try to increase the intensity and duration of your workouts a bit:** Make slight adjustments regularly during the program. You can create a program with high intensity and low intensity exercises, or gradually increase the time it takes to complete a session. For instance, if your total exercise session on Monday takes 10 minutes, increase it by two minutes on Wednesday and five minutes on Friday.
- **Journal your experience:** Journaling increases your focus, reduces stress, and allows you to pinpoint areas where improvement can be made. It also reminds you of your fitness goals and can give you something to look back on when you've completed the plan.

Aim to do five to seven exercises per day, and set the duration and number of reps for each exercise if needed. With that in mind, it's time to get into it.

YOUR DIY

YOUR DIY									
DAYS	TIME ON/ REST	REPS	EXERCISES						
MON									
TUES									
WED									
THURS									
FRI									
SAT									
SUN									

Key Takeaways

- Choose exercises that are enjoyable but also challenging.
- Try to remain accountable to yourself by journaling your experience with the fitness plan and seeing it to the end.
- You can join hands with your doctor to create a program that puts your current health needs into consideration.

Starting Strong

- Is creating your own workout plan something you'll consider doing again?
- What type of exercises do you favor most? Did that affect the way you made your plan?

CONCLUSION

Throughout this book, we've looked at aging, the various ways it can affect the body, and how exercise can positively change the health of a senior, giving them something to look forward to in the years to come. We've also looked at exercise in relation to sarcopenia, a common condition affecting older adults, and how nutrition and physical activity are connected to one another.

In the chapters that followed, we discussed ways to get started, the equipment you'll need, and how to keep going when there isn't enough motivation to get you out of bed. We took a deep dive into exercises for different parts of the body until we came to a place where you'll have to put your knowledge, motivation, and experience to the test in a workout program designed to get you started on your fitness journey and keep you going long after. To top it all off, you were able to create a program combining exercises you enjoy and those that challenge you.

As we draw to the close of this book, congratulations on taking the first step towards turning your health around by finishing it, because I'm certain that there were times you were tempted to give up on the entire idea of getting fit. As you continue to improve your health and body, pick up this book as many times as you need to, and continue to implement the principles you've learned. But it doesn't end there.

In the days to come, you'll be introduced to books intended to build upon your current success and increase your knowledge of some of the exercises we briefly touched on in this book such as stretching, resistance band training, balance exercises, and more. To be one of the first people to receive the books when they are released, join my email list, www.iaa.pub/fitness and we'll notify you as soon as they are available.

Keep striving for what you want, and enjoy living life on your own terms.

Thank you so much for reading Fitness For Seniors.

This book was written to provide helpful information to people, I hope you've learned that fitness can be improved at any age, that it's never too late to start, and that you'll use what you've learned in this book to build strength, improve balance as well as to look and feel years younger boosting your confidence!

I Have A Favor To Ask: Would you please take a couple of minutes to write a review of this book on Amazon? I'll be checking the reviews personally and your honest feedback will help me better help others on their fitness journey.

To Leave Me A Review:

- You can visit www.iaa.pub/review and you'll be automatically taken to Amazon to leave a review.
- You can also visit Amazon on your web browser, search for "*Fitness For Seniors 50, 60 and Beyond*" click the link for this book, scroll down, and click on "write a customer review."

Thank you, and I look forward to reading your comments!

REFERENCES

A quote by Jim Rohn. (n.d.). Www.goodreads.com; goodreads. https://www.goodreads.com/quotes/42751-motivation-is-what-gets-you-started-habit-is-what-keeps

Aging.com. (2017, December 4). *Elderly nutrition 101: 10 foods to keep you healthy*. Aging.com. https://aging.com/elderly-nutrition-101-10-foods-to-keep-you-healthy/

Allen, L. H. (2012). Vitamin B-12. *Advances in Nutrition*, *3*(1), 54–55. https://doi.org/10.3945/an.111.001370

Baron, K. G., Reid, K. J., & Zee, P. C. (2013). Exercise to Improve Sleep in Insomnia: Exploration of the Bidirectional Effects. *Journal of Clinical Sleep Medicine*, *9*(8), 819–824. https://doi.org/10.5664/jcsm.2930

Bernstein, M., & Munoz, N. (2012). Position of the Academy of Nutrition and Dietetics: Food and Nutrition for Older Adults: Promoting Health and Wellness. *Journal of the Academy of Nutrition and Dietetics*, *112*(8), 1255–1277. https://doi.org/10.1016/j.jand.2012.06.015

Bobroff, L. B. (2012). MyPlate for Older Adults. *EDIS*, *2012*(2). https://doi.org/10.32473/edis-fy1260-2011

Chaabene, H., Behm, D. G., Negra, Y., & Granacher, U. (2019). Acute Effects of Static Stretching on Muscle Strength and Power: An Attempt to Clarify Previous Caveats. *Frontiers in Physiology*, *10*. https://doi.org/10.3389/fphys.2019.01468

Chodzko-Zajko, W. J., Proctor, D. N., Fiatarone Singh, M. A., Minson, C. T., Nigg, C. R., Salem, G. J., & Skinner, J. S. (2009).

Exercise and Physical Activity for Older Adults. *Medicine & Science in Sports & Exercise*, *41*(7), 1510–1530. https://doi.org/10.1249/mss.0b013e3181a0c95c

Clemson, L., Fiatarone Singh, M. A., Bundy, A., Cumming, R. G., Manollaras, K., O'Loughlin, P., & Black, D. (2012). Integration of balance and strength training into daily life activity to reduce rate of falls in older people (the LiFE study): randomised parallel trial. *BMJ*, *345*(aug07 1), e4547–e4547. https://doi.org/10.1136/bmj.e4547

Deer, R. R., & Volpi, E. (2015). Protein intake and muscle function in older adults. *Current Opinion in Clinical Nutrition and Metabolic Care*, *18*(3), 248–253. https://doi.org/10.1097/mco.0000000000000162

Home | Dietary Guidelines for Americans. (n.d.). Www.dietaryguidelines.gov. https://www.dietaryguidelines.gov

Harvard Health Publishing. (2014, March 9). *Exercise and aging: Can you walk away from Father Time - Harvard Health*. Harvard Health; Harvard Health. https://www.health.harvard.edu/staying-healthy/exercise-and-aging-can-you-walk-away-from-father-time

Hughes, C. F., Ward, M., Hoey, L., & McNulty, H. (2013). Vitamin B12 and ageing: current issues and interaction with folate. *Annals of Clinical Biochemistry*, *50*(Pt 4), 315–329. https://doi.org/10.1177/0004563212473279

Inami, T. (2014). Long-term Stretching Program in Older Active Adults Increases Muscle Strength. *Journal of Exercise, Sports & Orthopedics*, *1*(2). https://doi.org/10.15226/2374-6904/1/2/00112

Irwin, M. L., Yasui, Y., Ulrich, C. M., Bowen, D., Rudolph, R. E., Schwartz, R. S., Yukawa, M., Aiello, E., Potter, J. D., & McTiernan, A. (2003a). Effect of exercise on total and intra-abdominal body fat in postmenopausal women: a randomized controlled trial. *JAMA*, *289*(3), 323–330. https://doi.org/10.1001/jama.289.3.323

Irwin, M. L., Yasui, Y., Ulrich, C. M., Bowen, D., Rudolph, R. E., Schwartz, R. S., Yukawa, M., Aiello, E., Potter, J. D., & McTiernan, A. (2003b). Effect of exercise on total and intra-abdominal body fat in postmenopausal women: a randomized controlled trial. *JAMA*, *289*(3), 323–330. https://doi.org/10.1001/jama.289.3.323

Kim, S. G., Yong, M. S., & Na, S. S. (2014). The Effect of Trunk Stabilization Exercises with a Swiss Ball on Core Muscle Activation in the Elderly. *Journal of Physical Therapy Science*, *26*(9), 1473–1474. https://doi.org/10.1589/jpts.26.1473

Lichtenstein, A. H., Rasmussen, H., Yu, W. W., Epstein, S. R., & Russell, R. M. (2008). Modified MyPyramid for Older Adults. *The Journal of Nutrition*, *138*(1), 5–11. https://doi.org/10.1093/jn/138.1.5

Lifer, H. S. (2007, July). *How and why to lose belly fat - AARP The Magazine*. Aarp.org; AARP. https://www.aarp.org/health/fitness/info-2007/belly_fat.html

McGavock, J. M., Hastings, J. L., Snell, P. G., McGuire, D. K., Pacini, E. L., Levine, B. D., & Mitchell, J. H. (2009). A Forty-Year Follow-Up of the Dallas Bed Rest and Training Study: The Effect of Age on the Cardiovascular Response to Exercise in Men. *The Journals of Gerontology Series A: Biological Sciences and Medical Sciences*, *64A*(2), 293–299. https://doi.org/10.1093/gerona/gln025

Peters, A. (2019, February 27). *Why Do We Crave Sweets When We're Stressed?* Scientificamerican.com; Scientific American. https://www.scientificamerican.com/article/why-do-we-crave-sweets-when-were-stressed/

Peterson, R., Lopez, O., Armstrong, M., & Getchius, T. (2017, December). Practice guideline update summary: Mild cognitive impairment: Report of the Guideline Development, Dissemination, and Implementation Subcommittee of the American Academy of Neurology. *Neurology, 90*(3). DOI:10.1212/WNL.0000000000004826. Researchgate.net; ResearchGate. https://www.researchgate.net/publication/322091224_Practice_guideline_update_summary_Mild_cognitive_impairment_Report_of_the_Guideline_Development_Dissemination_and_Implementation_Subcommittee_of_the_American_Academy_of_Neurology

Publishing, H. H. (2012, January 12). *The real-world benefits of strengthening your core*. Harvard Health. https://www.health.harvard.edu/healthbeat/the-real-world-benefits-of-strengthening-your-core

Szulc, P., Beck, T. J., Marchand, F., & Delmas, P. D. (2004). Low Skeletal Muscle Mass Is Associated With Poor Structural Parameters of Bone and Impaired Balance in Elderly Men-The MINOS Study. *Journal of Bone and Mineral Research*, *20*(5), 721–729. https://doi.org/10.1359/jbmr.041230

Thomas, R., Kenfield, S. A., Yanagisawa, Y., & Newton, R. U. (2021). Why exercise has a crucial role in cancer prevention, risk reduction and improved outcomes. *British Medical Bulletin*, *139*(1), 100–119. https://doi.org/10.1093/bmb/ldab019

USDA. (2020a). Dietary Guidelines for Americans 2020 -2025 Make Every Bite Count With the Dietary Guidelines. In *dietary guidelines.gov* (9th Edition, Chapter 4: Adults) (pp. 91–106). U.S. Department of Agriculture. https://www.dietaryguidelines.gov/sites/default/files/2021-03/Dietary_Guidelines_for_Americans-2020-2025.pdf

USDA. (2020b). Dietary Guidelines for Americans 2020 -2025 Make Every Bite Count With the Dietary Guidelines. In *dietaryguidelines.gov* (9th Edition Chapter 6: Older Adults) (pp. 121–130). U.S. Department of Agriculture. https://www.

dietaryguidelines.gov/sites/default/files/2021-03/Dietary_Guidelines_for_Americans-2020-2025.pdf

von Haehling, S., Morley, J. E., & Anker, S. D. (2010). An overview of sarcopenia: facts and numbers on prevalence and clinical impact. *Journal of Cachexia, Sarcopenia and Muscle*, *1*(2), 129–133. https://doi.org/10.1007/s13539-010-0014-2

Wallmann, H. W. (2009). Stretching and Flexibility in the Aging Adult. *Home Health Care Management & Practice*, *21*(5), 355–357. https://doi.org/10.1177/1084822309334073

Winchester, J. B., Nelson, A. G., Landin, D., Young, M. A., & Schexnayder, I. C. (2008). Static Stretching Impairs Sprint Performance in Collegiate Track and Field Athletes. *Journal of Strength and Conditioning Research*, *22*(1), 13–19. https://doi.org/10.1519/jsc.0b013e31815ef202

Wood, C. (1993). Mood change and perceptions of vitality: a comparison of the effects of relaxation, visualization and yoga. *Journal of the Royal Society of Medicine*, *86*(5), 254–258. https://pubmed.ncbi.nlm.nih.gov/8505745/

Printed in Great Britain
by Amazon

22656818R00093